Emaan Power

Copyright © *2019 Ariba Farheen*

First edition 2019

All rights reserved.

No part of this book may be reproduced or utilized in any form or by any means, electronic or mechanical, including photocopying and recording by any information storage and retrieval systems, without the written permission of the publisher

Author, **Ariba Farheen**
Designer, **Ryan Mahendra**

Published by **Emaan Power, Australia**

Website: www.emaanpower.com

Email: support@emaanpower.com

Facebook: www.facebook/emaanpower

Table of contents

Acknowledgement iii
Message for the readers ii

An Incredible Meeting And The Gift 1
    50 Prayers a day!!? But why? 5
    Does Allah need my prayer? 8

THE PROPHET'S WORRY 13

True Happiness 19

Why do we pray 22
    Make Allah your best friend forever 23
    The closest position to Allah (swt) 33
        A pit-stop 40
        What do we need to check during this pit-stop? 45
        True Story: When I was about to yell 46
        Another true story from my life 49
    Salah is a bath 51
    Follow your heart 54
    Salah is your armour 57
        Compare these two 61

Walking with an army of angels	62
Gratitude	72
War Horses	75
Is shaitan a Muslim?	82
Salah is a pillar of Islam	85
Who is a hypocrite?	86
Come to prayer, Come to success	95
Nag your parents!	102
Are you praying for your parents or for Allah (swt)?	103
True story: The double-edged dagger	106
Why does Allah want me to wake up so early?	115
Space rockets, salah and friendship	128
What is the source of your confidence?	141
Your report card	142
Do you want shaitan to urinate in your ear?	143
First check on the day of judgment	150

People who won't be able to bow down 152

Where will you be standing? 152

League of Musallin (those who pray) 153

Story of the lost camel 154

Would you like to see Allah (swt) 160

Do you have a time machine? 167

There are so many, it's okay if we miss one 170

If you really knew 172

Praying at school 175

Legs shaking with fear 176

Make a prayer buddy 181

Build your soldiers 182

Ask Allah (swt) for help 184

In the name of Allah, the most merciful, the most compassionate

Alhamdulillah, All of the praise and thanks belongs to Allah (swt) for allowing me to write this inspirational book for children.

May Allah (swt) put barakah in this work and in the lives of all those who read it.

May Allah (swt) forgive me for any shortcomings in this book and replace them with goodness.

May Allah (swt) guide the hearts of all those who read this book and give them the tawfique to pray consistently with excellence.

Acknowledgments

Alhamdulillah, who enabled me to write this book. I don't deserve to write about this incredible topic of Salah. It is only by the immense mercy of my Rabb that I have been able to complete this book.

JazakAllah Khair, May Allah reward all those who contributed to this book in various small and big ways and those who gave their precious time in reviewing it.

JazakAllah Khair, Faraaz A. Siddiqui, for his contributions to this book.

JazakAllah Khair, the children who shared their inspirational personal experiences with me.

May Allah (swt) reward all those parents who invest in this book for their children and the children who put in the time to read and improve themselves.

May Allah (swt) accept it from all of us

Message for the readers

Dear reader,

MashaAllah, that you have come across this book and decided to read it.

Do you think it was a mere coincidence that today you are reading this book?

If this book inspires you in any way, know that for sure that this is a gift from Allah (swt), **chosen for you**!

He is already calling you towards him.

May hundreds of angels surround you as you read this book.

May Allah (swt) reward you for every single second you spend reading this book.

Reflect on the reason you are reading this book. You are reading it to come closer to Allah (swt) and Allah knows that. He will surely give you what you hope to achieve from this book.

There are so many benefits and power in salah that it was impossible for me to cover it in this book. There was a lot more I wished I could have said and there is a lot more that there is for you to learn from what others have to teach about salah. So don't think of this book as the end, or reject it thinking, "I already know all about it," read it with the hope from – Al Alim, The All knower, to give you knowledge and guidance.

We are each other's way to Jannah 😊

I am so glad to have reached you, wherever in the world you are and I hope Allah (swt) re-unites us in Jannah. Then InshaAllah we will share more of our stories of salah 😊 😊

If you enjoy this book and are inspired by it, please do say a dua for me too in your next salah.

You can always write back and share your thoughts about the book with me by emailing support@emaanpower.com

A little about the author

Together we have done wonderful work to contribute to the world, such as building water wells in Somalia, Afghanistan, Bangladesh, sponsoring orphans, helping children living on streets, and much more.

It's been an exciting time and given me great happiness. However, I must confess there have been great challenges along the way.

But there was one thing I had that made everything easy and filled me with confidence – SALAH! My prayer, my meeting with Allah (swt).

Whenever I was headed in the wrong direction, doing something stupid, maybe even committing a sin, salah helped me come back to the right direction.

I love my salah and I can't imagine life without it. Alhamdulillah, All praise and thanks belongs to Allah, who gave us the gift of salah.

An Incredible Meeting and the Gift

During one of the most difficult days of his life, the Prophet Muhammad (saws) was taken on the greatest journey of his life. Angel Jibreel (pbuh) descended to Earth, with an animal from heaven called Buraq. Buraq was faster than the fastest rockets we know of, and it took the Prophet Muhammad (saws) to Palestine.

From there Angel Jibreel (pbuh) took the Prophet Muhammad (saws) to above the heavens and kept going higher and higher until they reached the point beyond which no one was allowed to go, not even Angel Jibreel (pbuh).

But today was a great day, the day of Isra and Miraj!

It was the day Allah (swt) had invited the creation He loves the most, Prophet Muhammad (pbuh), to a private meeting with Him.

So, Angel Jibreel (pbuh) told the Prophet Muhammad (saws) to proceed and the Prophet Muhammad (saws) proceeded until finally he was...

Right in front of Allah (swt)!

Yes! He was in front of Allah (swt). He had entered a meeting with Allah (swt)!!

Allah (swt) was right in front of him. The Prophet Muhammad (saws) could talk to Him. He was so close to Allah (swt) that between them was just a thin curtain of bright light. He couldn't see Allah (swt) but the Lord of the worlds was right in front of him!

WOW! Can you imagine that?

What would it be like to be right in front of Allah (swt)? What would it be like when Allah (swt) is turned towards you? What would it be like to be in a private meeting with Allah (swt), talking to Him, to be in front of Him? What would you do? What would you say? What would you ask for?

Just imagining myself in a meeting like this makes my heart beat faster!

What about you? Don't you wish you could also have such a meeting?!

Ahh… if only we could also have a meeting like this…

Hey, wait… Guess what?!

In that meeting, Allah (swt) gave the Prophet Muhammad (saws) a gift, a gift for his entire ummah.

The gift of Salah - a private meeting-time between you and Allah (swt) five times a day.

Just as the Prophet Muhammad (saws) was right in front of Allah (swt) that day, talking to Him, in a meeting with Him, in the same way, your Salah is your meeting with the Lord of the worlds, when Allah (swt) is right in front of you. He turns towards you, He is talking to you, and you are talking to Him. Salah is your private meeting-time with the Creator of this universe, the one who controls everything – Allah (swt)..

Interesting Fact

Every other command, such as for fasting, zakat, hajj, came down to earth through angel Jibreel (pbuh), except the command of prayer. For this Allah (swt) called Prophet Muhammad (saws) above the heavens, in a meeting with him, and then directly gave him this gift for his ummah. Why do you think that was?

So, remember the next time you are standing for your prayer; imagine yourself to be in the same way as the Prophet (saws) was that day. The Prophet Muhammad (saws) didn't see Allah (swt) in front of him that day, just like we also don't see Allah (swt) in front of us when we are praying. All he saw was light, and that is what you should imagine to be in front of you when you are praying – light in front of you. But know for sure in your heart that this is a meeting that can change your entire life – or rather I should say 'lives' (this one and the next one).

Let me ask you again. What would you do when you meet Allah (swt)? What would you say?

Would you be thinking about games? Movies? Homework? Friends?

50 Prayers a Day!!? But Why? 😮

In that meeting, Allah (swt) at first ordered 50 prayers per day. Can you imagine praying 50 times a day?! That would be like praying twice every hour!

When Prophet Mohammed (saws) was leaving, he met Musa (pbuh). Musa (pbuh) told him that this would be too much for his people and to go back and ask Allah (swt) to reduce it. So, Prophet Mohammed (saws) went back and requested Allah (swt) to reduce the amount, and Allah (swt) reduced it. But again Musa (pbuh) said this would still be too much and so the Prophet Muhammad (saws) went back and Allah (swt) reduced it again, and again, and again till... Allah (swt) reduced it to five times a day.

Think about it, though.

Why did Allah (swt) order 50? Didn't He know that He was later going to change it to five? That Prophet Muhammad (saws) was going to request that it be reduced? Of course, Allah (swt) knows everything. He knows the future, so He must have known. So why? Why didn't Allah (swt) just say five to start with?

Well, there could be many reasons, some that we may not understand now...

But here are some of my reflections.

1. We are capable of doing 50: Allah (swt) designed us. He knows what we're all capable of. He knows we could have done 50. It would have been hard but not impossible. The fact that Allah (swt) ordered 50 shows us we are actually capable of praying 50 times a day, but now we only have to do 5. That is so much easier than what we are actually capable of; not hard at all!

2. Mercy of Allah (swt): It shows us the mercy of Allah (swt). Allah (swt) changed the number of prayers from 50 to five but... HE DID NOT CHANGE THE REWARD! Although you only pray five times a day, Allah (swt) rewards you like you are praying 50 times! SubhanAllah! How generous is Allah (swt)! He loves rewarding you. Do you see how much He appreciates your good actions?! Is there anyone in the world who appreciates you like this, who appreciates you as much? Allah (swt) is Ash Shakur, Ash Shakir.

All this when... Allah (swt) didn't even have to reward us for our prayers. Could Allah have just ordered us to pray and said there will be zero reward? Sure, but Allah is Ar Raheem so, even though he doesn't have to, he still rewards us!

Do you think there could be more reasons? I would love to hear your thoughts; you can email me at ariba@emaanpower.com

يَـٰٓأَيُّهَا ٱلنَّاسُ أَنتُمُ ٱلْفُقَرَآءُ إِلَى ٱللَّهِ ۖ وَٱللَّهُ هُوَ ٱلْغَنِىُّ ٱلْحَمِيدُ ﴿١٥﴾

O mankind, you are those in need of Allah, while Allah is the Free of Need, the Praiseworthy. (35:15)

DOES ALLAH NEED MY PRAYER?

This is a real picture taken by Hubble telescope of a legion of galaxies. Did you know there are more stars in the universe than there are specks of dust on Earth?

In this picture, you can see many galaxies, each one with millions of gigantic stars, solar systems, and planets. Somewhere in one of the galaxies in the universe is our solar system and in that is a planet we call Earth. Earth is not even as small as a speck of dust compared to the entire universe.

In Ayatul Kursi, Allah tells us that His Throne is greater than the entire universe. Allah is greater than the entire universe.

How small is the Earth in front of Allah (swt)? Is it even a dot?

Then what about us? What are we in front of Allah? Not even a dot. How could anyone think that Allah would need anything from them? It's like the dot saying, "Allah needs me." Seriously!

Allah needs my prayer

Why would He? Everything we have is given to us by Allah (swt). Whether we pray or not makes no difference to Allah (swt).

Allah (swt) does not need us to pray to Him, love Him, praise Him or thank Him.

He could easily destroy us all in a second and create a new, even bigger planet and new people in it.

We are the ones who NEED Him. We need His love. We need his help.

We need to thank Him, so we can be happy in our lives. We need to praise Him to strengthen our own selves and, even though we are not even a dot in front of him, He still appreciates our good actions, He still answers you when you call on him. Most of all, He grants you his love when you strive for it!

Allah is Ar Rahman, the most merciful. Allah is Al Wadud, the most loving.

If you want to learn more about this you can watch my video "How big is Allah?" on Emaan Power channel on YouTube

The Salah is every Muslim's personal, private meeting with Allah (swt) that we all get five times a day. Five times a day, you have a private meeting with the Lord of the worlds, the one who owns everything and who created everything, the one who has power over everyone and everything.

He has a private meeting with you; just you. In your Salah, it's just you and Him. The Lord of the worlds has a private meeting booked with you five times a day (Do you rush to it?).

This, if you really think about it, is incredible. Is there anybody in the world who gives you that much importance? Would a president, prime minister, king give you even one appointment?

Even your mom and dad… Do they turn to you, five times a day, and say "Okay, I'm going to sit down; I'll turn to you and just listen to you." But Allah (swt) does! Five times a day, every single day, He is turned to you.

This is so powerful. The most powerful one turns to you five times a day!

Are you taking advantage of this meeting, or are you turning up late?

As soon as you say, "Allahu akbar" in your prayer, Allah turns towards you and He remains turned to you until you finish your Salah or you turn away.

How do we turn away in the middle of our Salah? Someone might start looking here and there, or they might start thinking about other things. For example, somebody is praying and they're thinking, "Hmm, what will be my strategy in Minecraft?" Then their heart has turned away, and so then Allah will also turn away from them. The Salah is carrying on, the meeting is carrying on, but this extra favor you had from Allah (swt) is gone. But, otherwise, five times a day, if you are in your prayer, Allah (swt) is in a private meeting with you, turned towards you.

If the only thing that you changed in your life today was to improve the way you were praying, to excel in your prayers, then your entire life would change. You would be a much stronger person and definitely a much more successful person.

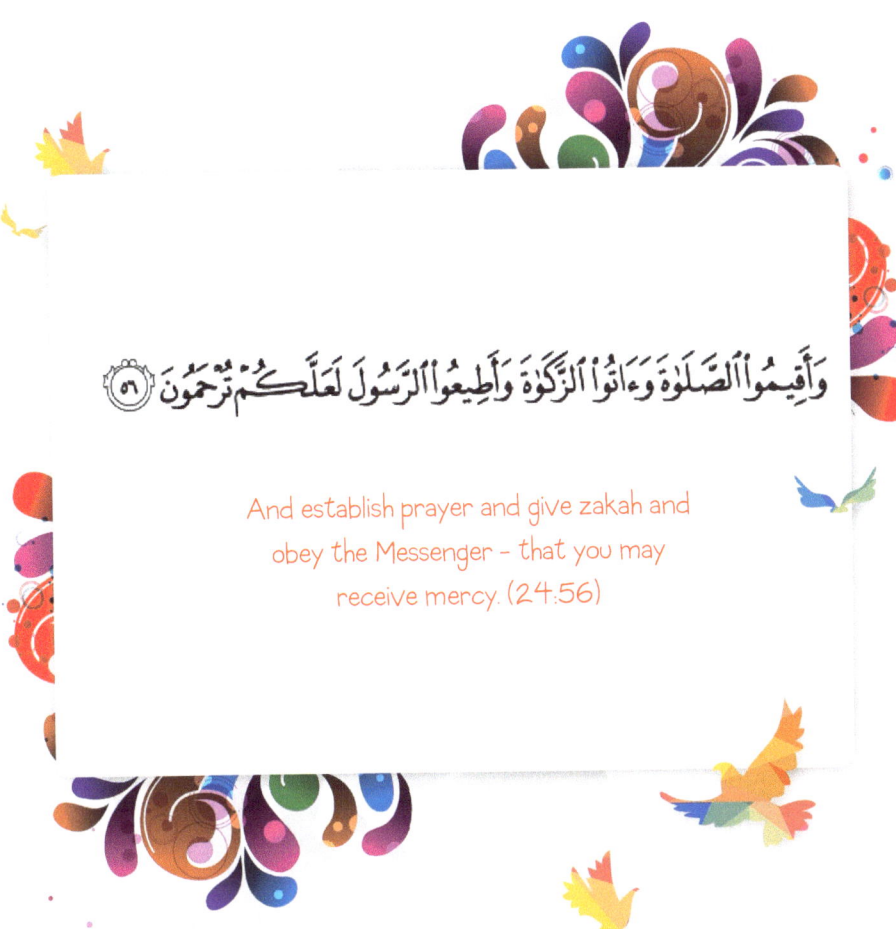

وَأَقِيمُوا۟ ٱلصَّلَوٰةَ وَءَاتُوا۟ ٱلزَّكَوٰةَ وَأَطِيعُوا۟ ٱلرَّسُولَ لَعَلَّكُمْ تُرْحَمُونَ ۝

And establish prayer and give zakah and obey the Messenger - that you may receive mercy. (24:56)

Alhamdulillah, for allowing us to meet him and worship him salah 5 times a day!

THE PROPHET'S WORRY

Prophet's prayer was obviously excellent. Did he just pray five times a day? No, he prayed more than five times a day. One of the prayers he used to pray every night was the tahajjud prayer – the prayer after midnight, in the last third of the night, before Fajr. He used to wake up and pray for a really long time. Why? Because he loved it. He enjoyed it so much. He loved talking to Allah (swt), meeting with Allah (swt) in his prayer.

Towards the end of his life, the Prophet Muhammad (saws) had become extremely sick.

One day he got up and asked, "Have the Muslims prayed?" He was told, "No, Ya Rasulallah, they are waiting

Muslims' Badge of Honour

Tahajjud is a prayer in the last third of the night, when Allah (swt) comes down to the lowest heaven and says, "Is there anyone asking for anything, so I can give it to them?" "Is there anyone seeking forgiveness, so I can forgive them?"

Most of the people are sleeping, but a few are awake, standing in prayer, in the darkness ad silence of the night. There are Muslims all over the world, who leave their sleep, their comfortable beds, and stand up in prayer while everyone is in deep sleep. Can you imagine how successful those muslims will be? They are the honored ones! As Jibreel Alahisalaam said once to the Prophet Muhammad (saws), "Your honor is in the right prayer." The solutions to many of your problems, are in your night prayer! Will you be among those special muslims? Will you earn this honour?

for you." So, he said, "Okay! Bring a bucket of water. I will wash up and then we will go and pray." So they brought a bucket of water and he tried to get up, but he collapsed and fainted. Once again, when he woke, the first thing he asked was not to give him water, food, medicine; no, he asked, "Have the Muslims prayed?" He was told, "No, Ya Rasulallah, they are waiting for you." So, he said, "Okay! Bring a bucket of water. I will wash up and then we will go and pray." So they brought a bucket of water and he tried to get up, but he collapsed and fainted. Then again a third time he woke up, clearly very weak, but the first thing he asked was, "Have the Muslims prayed?"

He was told, "No Ya Rasulallah, they are waiting for you." So, once again he said, "Okay. Bring a bucket of water. I will wash up and then we will go and pray." He kept trying but he couldn't; so, finally, he asked Abu Bakr (raa) to come and lead the prayer, so everyone's prayers were not delayed.

We can see from this how much pain he was in. He was not even able to stand up. Yet he was extremely concerned about the Salah of the Muslims. "Have the Muslims prayed?" he kept asking and kept trying to lead the prayer, until he collapsed again and again. Can you imagine how worried our beloved Prophet Muhammad (saws) was for your prayer?

The days kept passing and the Prophet Muhammad (saws) kept getting sicker and sicker. He got so sick in his final days that he couldn't move, he couldn't even move his mouth enough to brush his own teeth. He was in great pain, perhaps the greatest pain anyone has ever experienced.

But even in this pain, there was just one word he kept repeating again and again – "As Salah, As Salah."

Of course, there must have been a lot of things the Prophet wanted to remind the people of before he was gone, but there was one he kept repeating again and again: "As Salah, As Salah." This is the one he was most worried about. "Will they pray after I'm gone? Will they forget to pray?" He knew that, if the Muslims held on to their prayer, they would be fine, they would be strong and successful. But, if they left their prayers, then of course they would be extremely weak, they would lose their Islam, their enemies would overcome them.

Then one day, just a day or two before he died, the Prophet Muhammad (saws) suddenly felt better! He could stand up! He stood up and opened the curtain of his door. The Prophet's room was connected with the masjid. So, when he opened the door, he could look in the masjid. He saw hundreds of people, standing in rows in…SALAH.

He was so happy to see them praying, he just stood there looking at them, smiling :)

Would you have liked to have seen the beautiful smile on the face of the Prophet?

He was truly happy to see that they were holding on to their prayer. Even when he was not there to remind them, they were holding on to their prayer. The Prophet Muhammad (saws) was very happy.

Can you imagine how happy he will be when he meets YOU!

When you tell him your name is... and I lived more than 1000 years after he died, in the 21st century, and I have prayed all my life, exactly the same way as you taught us.

WOW!! What an awesome day that would be!

Prophet Muhammad (saws) would be very happy to meet you.

He would be very happy to meet you, InshaAllah!

He might give you a big hug, invite you to drink from his river, invite you to his palaces, eat delicious Jannah food with him! He would love you so very much. You could go for a walk with him in Jannah, where the sand is like white powder of perfume, lights are of pearls. You could sit with him and hear all about his life from himself. Tell him about your stories, all the times he inspired you and all the sunnahs that you used to do to follow him.

"It is a river that Allah has given to me in Paradise. Its mud is musk and its water is whiter than milk and sweeter than honey. Birds with necks like the necks of camels drink from it." [Ahmad]

InshaAllah, that day is coming soon!

So we know the Prophet Muhammad (saws) would be pleased to know about your prayers. We know Allah (swt) is pleased to see you pray. But who else? Who else do you know is truly happy to see you pray?

Hmmm... well, think about it. Who gave you this book? Who reminds you to pray all the time? Who taught you to pray?

Yes! That's right, your parents!

True Happiness

True happiness is what your mom and dad get by seeing you pray – and not after they have told you, "Get up, pray; get up, pray..." like a hundred times. No, that's not what I'm talking about. I mean when you get up by yourself, get ready with your wudu and you pray without even being reminded. 👍

That is the true happiness you give your parents: when you become in charge of your own prayer, when you take responsibility for your own prayer.

This is happiness not like any other happiness. That is, like, true happiness and peace of heart.

Have you guys ever made gifts and things to make your parents happy?

Whatever gift you have given them, the happiness of that is like nothing – not even 1% – compared to the happiness they will get when they see you praying well, five times a day. When you pray right on time without delay, by yourselves. When you pray good quality prayers, concentrating, having a good connection with Allah (swt).

Oh, wow! That feeling for your parents, it will make your mom and dad so happy.

Whatever worries they have about you, whatever stress – a lot of that will also go away.

Then they will know, "My daughter will be okay, my son will be okay. They are praying. They are with Allah (swt). Allah (swt) is going to protect them." That's the greatest joy and happiness you can give your parents.

Do you want to give your parents the gift of Paradise?

Every time you pray, not only does Allah (swt) reward you massively, but Allah (swt) will also reward your parents. *(Don't worry! He is not taking your good deeds and giving them away. He is giving to you and additionally giving to your parents as well.)* So, not only are you helping yourself every time you pray, you are also helping your parents go to Jannah. You are literally saving them from fire! 😁

Giving them a gift of Paradise, every single prayer! 🎁 🎁

But what if you don't pray?

If you don't pray, and your parents let you get away with that – if they don't care whether you pray or not – then it's possible that Allah (swt) will hold them accountable. Allah (swt) will ask them and hold them accountable for it.

If you are a child, below the age of maturity, then you will not earn any sins for not praying. Allah (swt) is not going to punish you. There might be still really negative consequences for you, for not praying – we will talk about them later – but Allah (swt) is not going to punish you or be angry with you. But if you are this age and your parents don't care whether you are praying or not, then Allah (swt) may hold them accountable for that!

Be the reason for your parents to be in Jannah!

Why Do We Pray

There are hundreds of reasons why we pray, but here we are going to look at a few. Then you can reflect and discover some on your own

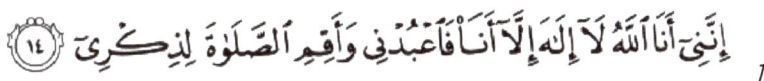 Indeed, I am Allah. There is no deity except Me, so worship Me and establish prayer for My remembrance.

The number 1 reason we pray is because Allah (swt) commanded us to. He is our Rabb and we must obey Him without any hesitation.

"We hear and we obey."

Make Allah Your Best Friend Forever

Do you have a best friend? Do you share things with them? Of course, you do!

If two people don't like talking to each other, do you think they could be best friends? No way!

We love talking to our friends, sharing things with them. Similarly, if you want to make Allah (swt) your best friend forever, your BFF, you can do that by talking to Him all the time! In fact, Allah (swt) can be the friend who is far better and closer than any other friend.

Imagine two girls, Sarah and Maryam, they are best friends and love each other. One day when Sarah wakes up in the morning, she calls Maryam

Then at 1 PM, Sarah calls Maryam again

Then at 4 PM, Sarah calls Maryam again

Then at 6 PM, Sarah calls Maryam again.

Then at 8 PM, Sarah calls Maryam again.

Lol! Didn't that get boring/annoying to even read? Imagine being in Maryam's place!

What if Sarah does this all over again the next day? Do you think Maryam would want to be Sarah's friend anymore? No way!

But now imagine that, instead of calling Maryam every few hours, Sarah calls on Allah and shares everything with Allah (swt)

Sarah starts her day with Fajr, thanks to Allah (swt) and makes dua to Allah (swt) for her day. Tells Allah (swt) that she is nervous about her speech, asks Allah (swt) for help. At 1 PM, Dhuhr time, she prays at school and tells Allah (swt) all about how her day has been, thanks to Allah (swt) for helping her in her speech. At 4 PM, Asr time, she tells Allah (swt) about the girls gossiping, how hurt she feels, asks him for help. At maghrib, again she talks to Allah (swt) and makes dua for a new phone. At Isha, before going to sleep, she again talks to Allah (swt) and tells Him all about her day and makes dua for tomorrow to go well.

Now who is Sarah's best friend?

Yes! Allah (swt)!

And Allah (swt) will never get annoyed of hearing Sarah. In fact, the more she talks to Allah (swt), the more He loves to hear from her.

The more she remembers Allah (swt), the more Allah (swt) will remember her.

Moreover, unlike our human friends, when she asks Allah (swt) for help, Allah (swt) can always help her!

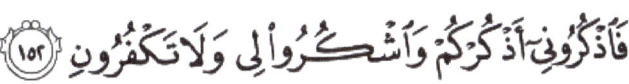

So remember Me; I will remember you. And be grateful to Me and do not deny Me.

There is this person who talks to Allah (swt) every few hours in Salah: First thing when they wake up in the morning; at school; then in evening again they are talking to Allah (swt); and, again praying to Allah (swt) before going to bed. Whatever problems they have – somebody bullied them, somebody hurt them, they have too much homework or they really want a new Xbox or a new iPhone, whatever – they are asking Allah (swt) constantly. How powerful is this person?! This person is in direct connection with the Lord of the universe, every few hours. You don't want to mess with this person!

Alhamdulillah, for allowing us to talk to him directly, meet him and worship him salah 5 times a day!

Then there is this other person who sometimes prays, sometimes doesn't pray, only sometimes talks to Allah (swt).

Do you think these two people can ever be the same? No. Of course, they can't!

Do you think this second person has taken Allah (swt) as a friend? Do you think this person even has a lot of love for Allah (swt) in their heart?

You could be that strong person, who has Allah (swt) as your best friend, if only you improved your Salah five times a day!

Whatever is happening with you – maybe somebody said something to you that was a little mean, you're feeling hurt about it and you can't tell anybody, or if you tell your parents they are like, "It's not a big deal, it's ok," but you are still feeling bad about it – talk to Allah (swt) in your prayer, talk to Allah (swt) about it.

Even though Allah (swt) knows everything that's happening with you, you can still talk to Allah (swt), and He loves to hear from you. Moreover, whatever you need, whatever problems, whatever is the solution to your problems, all Allah (swt) has to say is "Be!" and it will be. So why don't you talk to Allah (swt) about it? You know Allah has the solution for everything, so why are you not asking him for every little thing?

When in salah should you talk to Allah about your problems and requests? Find out in the next section...

وَٱسْتَعِينُوا۟ بِٱلصَّبْرِ وَٱلصَّلَوٰةِ ۚ وَإِنَّهَا لَكَبِيرَةٌ إِلَّا عَلَى ٱلْخَٰشِعِينَ ﴿٤٥﴾

And seek help through patience and prayer, and indeed, it is difficult except for the humbly submissive [to Allah] (2:45)

The Closest Position to Allah (swt)

If you really, really want to be close to Allah (swt), what do you do?

Take a rocket ship, go into space and pray there. Is that right?

NOOOO!

You don't have to go to space to be close to Allah (swt). You don't have to become an astronaut. That's ridiculous!

You don't need to go up; you need to go down on the floor with your head in prostration.

The lowest position.

Prostration or sujuud is the position in which a human being is closest to Allah (swt).

Why? Because it is the humblest position.

What's the top part of your body? Well, unless you have horns, it must be your head.

What is the lowest part of your body? Your feet. In sujuud, you have made your head equal to your feet, put them both on the floor, where people walk!

Even if you use the prayer mat, it is still the floor. We don't normally go about putting our heads on the floor. The highest, proudest part of your body – your head – in your sujuud, you put it on the floor, where people walk!

A Muslim bows their head ONLY for Allah (swt). We do not bow our heads down for anyone except Allah (swt).

Allah is our only Master and the only one who completely owns us.

Sujuud is the humblest position. It is the lowest position you can be in and it is the most powerful position.

You are closest to Allah (swt) in this position!

Notice every limb of your body is bowing down, it's bent down in its own way, even your toes.

And...

Even your heart!

And with all your desires, hopes and wishes are all submitting to Allah (swt)

Sujuud is like the peak of your salah, the best part of your salah.

In every salah make sure, that this is the best part of your salah.

With your body language, you are saying that "I am the lowest, I submit to you and you are the highest, and you are Almighty."

> **TIP:** Try not to get up from your sujuud until you feel in your heart "I'm nothing in front of you, O Allah. You are my master, You own me. I will do everything You tell me to do. I submit myself to You. I am your slave." Once you get this feeling of total submission and humility in your heart, only then should you get up from your sujuud.

Now, this is the closest you can be to Allah (swt); so, what else should you do? This is the best time to make dua! In your Salah, Allah (swt) is turned to you, and now you are in the closest position to Allah (swt). This is one of the best times to make dua. Ask Allah (swt) for whatever you want. In your prostration, you can make dua in English or in whatever language you like. Ask

Him for what you want in prostration in your prayer – new computer, good grades, Xbox, good friends… whatever you want!

Alhamdulillah, for teaching us to prostrate to him, allowing us to humble ourselves and come close to him through this way.

قُلْ إِنَّ صَلَاتِي وَنُسُكِي وَمَحْيَايَ وَمَمَاتِي لِلَّهِ رَبِّ ٱلْعَٰلَمِينَ ﴿١٦٢﴾

Say, "Indeed, my prayer, my rites of sacrifice, my living and my dying are for Allah, Lord of the worlds. (6:162)

A pit stop

Have you ever played a car-racing game or watched a real car race?

Then you must know what is a pit stop is.

During the car race, especially if it's a long one, the cars actually take a detour, DURING THE RACE, and go to the pit stops, where they come to a total stop. All this is happening while the other cars are still racing! Why? Why does the car come to a total stop in the middle of the race?

A pit- stop is short stop where the car goes to get checked, refreshed, or re-energiszed. There are a lot of people in the pit stop who quickly come and check the car, refuel it, change the tires, check anything else that might be going wrong, and then the car goes back into the race. All refreshed, refueled and re-energizsed.

Imagine if there is a driver who says, "No way, I am not making a pit stop. I don't have any time to waste. I am already in first place, I don't need to stop."

Do you think this driver can ever win the race?

NO! Of course not. He will probably go…

The tires might get really hot and burst. The car might run out of fuel and then stop in the middle of the track, and then another car might hit it.

Or something else might go wrong...

So, basically, it would be a really dumb decision not to stop at the pits and check everything, refresh everything. He saved a few minutes seconds by not making a pit stop but, in the end, he lost the race and hurt himself.

Salah is your pit stop! It is your checkpoint!

We might be very busy during the day – lots of activities, work, homework, school, things you want to do, this or that – but then, in the middle of our busy day, come these five pits stops, checking points – Salah!

This is when you check yourself. This is where you re-energize yourself.

If you don't stop at these five pit stops, you will never win the race to heaven.

There might be somebody who thinks, "Actually I don't pray, but my life is pretty ok without it." It's kind of like that driver. That driver might keep winning for a little while longer but, in the end, he is going to go kaboom – a disaster. That's how the life of someone who decides to skip prayers will be. They think, "I'm fine, I don't need to pray." But they are actually going towards big massive disasters in their life. Shaitan has laid down traps for them but, because they never check, they don't even realize they have already started going down the wrong road. Sure, things might seem fine now, but soon they will have massive problems in their lives and then what will they do? If only they had prayed, they could have protected themselves from all of what is going to deeply hurt them, and they could have kept winning!

What do we need to check during this pit stop?

What do you check in your prayer? You check how you are doing so far and correct what you might be doing wrong, for example:

- How am I doing so far in my day? Have I been wasting all my time?
- Have I been rude to someone today? My parents, my siblings, friends, or anyone else?

  - Ask Allah (swt) for forgiveness and help you be a better person.
  - Ask Allah (swt) to give you strength to be nicer to them and to apologize to them.

- What sins have I committed today? Better ask Allah (swt) for forgiveness right now before the sins start taking you down, before they start rotting your heart.
- Have I done any good deeds today? Reflect on how you can increase in some good today.

  - Can you help someone, share something, do something to make someone happy?

Alhamdulillah, for allowing us to check ourselves and seek his guidance five times a day in salah. *(I would have surely messed up a lot more without it)*

True Story: When I was about to yell

One day I was at work. One of my employees used to always make lots of mistakes. This day, I gave him a task and told him exactly what to do and what NOT to do. This was a very important task. I explained the task to him in detail and told him to make sure to do it as I had told him, otherwise we would be in a lot of trouble.

Anyway, a little while later, he came back and told me what he had done. Guess what, he had done exactly what I told him NOT to do. I was so annoyed. I thought, today I am going to yell at him so badly and I am going to fire him. But then I looked at the time and it was Asr prayer time. So, I thought: okay, I will go pray and then come back and yell at him!

 I went, did my wudu, did my Salah, bowed down to Allah (swt), asked him for forgiveness for my mistakes.

Then, I came back... Do you think I was still as angry as I was before?

No! Of course not!

The prayer had completely calmed me down. I remembered my own mistakes and decided to forgive him, hoping Allah (swt) would forgive me too when I make dumb mistakes.

This is just one small example of how prayer saved me from committing a sin and maybe causing many other problems that could have come up from my yelling at him at work.

Just like that, it might be that someday your sibling is annoying you a lot; maybe they did something bad to you. Then you think: I am going to teach them a lesson today and take my revenge. But then Salah time comes, and you go and pray. Do you think after you come back, you will still be as angry?

Of course not! Your prayer will calm you, make you stronger and more patient.

Before Prayer

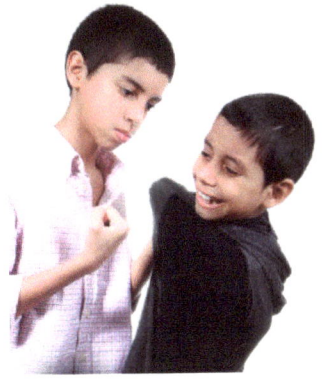

After Prayer

Another True Story from My Life

Similarly, a long time ago, I didn't used to wear Hijab. During the day, I thought about it sometimes but not that much. But whenever I went to pray, and I would prostrate to Allah (swt) and think "Ya, Allah, I submit to you, I will do everything You tell me to do." Then I would remember I am not actually doing everything Allah (swt) has told me to do. I am not telling the truth. I am refusing to wear the hijab every day.

What was happening? The prayer was helping me check myself, it was helping me check my emaan, it was helping me check any sins I was involved in, and it was helping me correct my mistakes.

In my sujuud I realized that, in order to completely submit to Allah (swt), to be true in my sujuud, I would have to obey Allah (swt) and put on the hijab. I then decided to leave behind everything else that worried me and put on my Hijab! Alhamdulillah!

I used to make dua in my sujuud because, remember, that's when dua is very powerful, to ask Allah (swt) to make it easy for me to wear the hijab and – Alhamdulillah! – now I love wearing it.

So, use your prayer to check yourself and re-energize your emaan, strengthen it. Make lots of dua, seek forgiveness for your mistakes, power up yourself up and get whatever help you need, every few hours, and – InshaAllah – the race to the highest Jannah will then be a piece of cake for you!

- Your Salah will not let you stray far away from Allah (swt).
- Your prayer is the proof of your love for Allah (swt).
- The strength of your prayer is the strength of your relationship with Allah (swt).

إِنَّمَا يُرِيدُ ٱلشَّيْطَٰنُ أَن يُوقِعَ بَيْنَكُمُ ٱلْعَدَٰوَةَ وَٱلْبَغْضَآءَ فِى ٱلْخَمْرِ وَٱلْمَيْسِرِ وَيَصُدَّكُمْ عَن ذِكْرِ ٱللَّهِ وَعَنِ ٱلصَّلَوٰةِ ۖ فَهَلْ أَنتُم مُّنتَهُونَ ﴿٩١﴾

Satan only wants to cause between you animosity and hatred through intoxicants and gambling and to avert you from the remembrance of Allah and from prayer. So will you not desist? (5:91)

Salah Is a Bath

The Prophet (saws) said Salah is like taking a bath: It washes your sins.

All of your minor sins will be washed away every time you go for prayer, InshaAllah.

What about a person who doesn't pray? They would be stinking with sins because they haven't taken their bath and their heart is rotting inside, they just don't see it yet. Sins are toxic to our souls. We do commit sins all the time and we need to wash them off ourselves all the time. The person who doesn't pray, his heart gets diseased due to the toxicity of the sins he has done and not washed away.

Sins don't just earn punishment for us in heaven. Every single sin has evil consequences in our lives and on our hearts. It hurts us in some way or other.

Sins make our hearts darker and darker. Every time we commit a sin, a dark spot comes in our heart and the more we do it the more it grows.

The darker someone's heart is, the more they would like to do bad things, hurt others and commit even worse sins.

The purer someone's heart is, the more they would love to do good things.

Salah is the bath that can wash it off, at least, your minor sins. So, make sure you have a nice bath five times a day and don't stink with the sins!

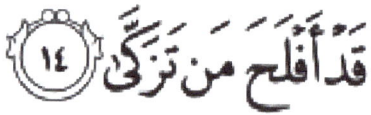

"He has certainly succeeded who purifies himself" (87:14)

Alhamdulillah, for allowing us to worship him in salah and cleaning our heart and washing sins through it. *(I don't even want to think how disgusting my heart would have been without it.)*

Follow Your Heart

Should you always follow your heart?

Wouldn't life be so much fun if you could just always follow your heart, do what your heart was telling you to?

InshaAllah, we can live this way, if our heart is pure and guided. Then, InshaAllah, it will only command us to do good, only desire good. Salah is going to help keep your heart guided!

Every prayer begins with a dua for guidance – Surah Fatiha. You are asking Allah (swt) to guide you to the right path and help you walk on it.

Every well prayed Salah puts light in your heart, to help you distinguish right from wrong, so you see things clearly.

While others may be far more confused, is this action right? Should I go to the party? Should I eat this? Should I lie? Should I do this or that?

You will, InshaAllah, have much more clarity, because your heart is guided! InshaAllah, then you can just follow your heart!

You will increase immensely in good deeds automatically because your heart is constantly going to command you to do good deeds.

To fill your heart with the light of An-Nur, make sure you fill your life with excellent prayers!

Alhamdulillah, for allowing us to continuously seek guidance from him five times a day every day. *(I must say without it, I would have surely forgotten on many days and would have been very lost.)*

Salah Is Your Armor

ٱتْلُ مَآ أُوحِىَ إِلَيْكَ مِنَ ٱلْكِتَٰبِ وَأَقِمِ ٱلصَّلَوٰةَ ۖ إِنَّ ٱلصَّلَوٰةَ تَنْهَىٰ عَنِ ٱلْفَحْشَآءِ وَٱلْمُنكَرِ ۗ وَلَذِكْرُ ٱللَّهِ أَكْبَرُ ۗ وَٱللَّهُ يَعْلَمُ مَا تَصْنَعُونَ ﴿٤٥﴾

"Verily, As-Salat prevents from Al-Fahsha'and Al-Munkar" (29:45)

Salah protects you from the Shaitaan. It protects you from committing sins. If you are praying five times a day, then Shaitaan really has not much power against you. You check yourself five times a day, how will he trap you? You have a meeting with your Protector, the Lord of the universe, five times a day; how will Shaitaan deceive you? With every well prayed Salah, you get stronger and stronger and he gets weaker and weaker against you.

You might still do some sins, minor sins, and, InshaAllah, they will be washed off next time you pray. But the big sins, the major sins, InshaAllah, you will not get involved in them. You will be so close to Allah (swt), that you would hate even the thought of doing major sins.

You check yourself five times a day and you will not go down the wrong road because you are keeping yourself in check. You're not like, "I don't know where I'm going, I'm just doing whatever." You cannot get lost. Allah (swt) is guiding you. Five times a day you are making dua for Allah (swt) to guide you to be like the best and most successful human beings.

> Guard your Salah and your Salah will guard you!

Even when Shaitaan comes and whispers things to you, he is not going to be able to fool you or deceive you, because your Salah is protecting you.

Now tell me: If a Muslim doesn't even pray, do you think they have strong armor? Do they even have any armor?

No, they don't. It's easy for Shaitaan to trap them in any kind of major sins. They will keep going down the wrong road and won't even realize it.

They don't go to their meetings with Allah (swt) five times a day. They think they don't need it, that they are strong enough without it. In reality, their soul is weak and is getting weaker and weaker.

Compare These Two

Adam, who prays five times a day, excellent quality prayers. He is guarded by his Salah. He is receiving the protection of the Lord of the worlds. He is constantly receiving the great blessings because of his prayer, making everything in his life easier.

Sughi, on the other hand, thinks he doesn't need his prayer. He doesn't have time and is too lazy to pray. How weak is he? How alone is he? He has forgotten about Allah (swt). He thinks he doesn't need Allah (swt). How lonely and weak do you think is Sughi?

The fact is that Allah is still protecting him, providing for him, that's why he is alive. BUT, the protection, the blessings Adam has are many times greater than what Sughi has from Allah (swt).

Walking with an Army of Angels

When Adam walks to school after praying Fajr on time, doing dhikr on his way, he is walking with an army of angels with him. Angels walking with him, making dua for him, showering blessings on him, inspiring him with good suggestions, protecting him from harm.

On the other hand, when Sughi walks to school, he is just alone. He has only himself to rely on, because he said he doesn't need Allah (swt).

No matter what kind of day he is having, no matter where in the world he is, five times a day Adam enters a meeting with Allah (swt). Allah (swt) turns towards Adam. Allah (swt) and Adam are in a private meeting. No matter how big his problems are, Adam remembers that he can rely on Allah (swt), the Lord of the universe. All Allah (swt) has to say is BE and it will be. So, he remains patient and goes through his tests while trusting Allah (swt) and doing the best deeds he can.

Will Adam never have any problems in his life?

It's not like Adam will never get into any problems or difficulties. Definitely he will. *(Even the Prophets have hardships.)* He might even face challenges greater than others because he is stronger than others. But no matter what happens, as long Allah (swt) is protecting him, nothing - absolutely nothing - can actually harm him or hurt him. He might be sad for a little while, hurt for a little while, but eventually he is going to be even stronger, happier and more successful. No matter how big the load of his problems, it will be lightened for him, because Allah is helping him.

As long as he is praying good quality prayers regularly, he will always come out to be the winner in the end!

However, Sughi has to face all challenges by himself.

Is there anyone at all who can always be there with him?

Will his friends or parents always be able to help him?

Is there anyone he can always count on or rely on? No, because he chose not to believe in and rely on Allah (swt).

He has to carry the whole burden of his worries and problems on his own. How will he deal with them? Of course, he is going to be much weaker and, in the end, get defeated by the devil.

وَأْمُرْ أَهْلَكَ بِالصَّلَوٰةِ وَاصْطَبِرْ عَلَيْهَا ۖ لَا نَسْـَٔلُكَ رِزْقًا ۖ نَّحْنُ نَرْزُقُكَ ۗ وَالْعَاقِبَةُ لِلتَّقْوَىٰ ﴿١٣٢﴾

And strive for Allah with the striving due to Him. He has chosen you and has not placed upon you in the religion any difficulty. [It is] the religion of your father, Abraham. Allah named you "Muslims" before [in former scriptures] and in this [revelation] that the Messenger may be a witness over you and you may be witnesses over the people. So establish prayer and give zakah and hold fast to Allah. He is your Protector; and excellent is the Protector, and excellent is the helper. (20:132)

Alhamdulillah, for allowing us to meet him and pray to him five times a day and making salah a protection for us.

What about somebody who prays but only prays a little bit?

Or someone who prays but is always late or in a hurry to get it over with?

Or someone who prays but is always thinking about something else while they are praying?

Do they have any armor?

Maybe a little bit, since they at least pray.

What happens if you have little or too-small armor and the enemy keeps attacking you? What will happen to that armor? It will break and fall apart.

That means Shaitaan will keep attacking them and, because they have weak armor or weak prayer, it's likely that soon they will completely stop praying.

Except...

Except if someone has weak armor but they are constantly trying to rebuild it, make it stronger, then it's possible that before the enemy defeats them they build their strong armor. But for that, you need to be vigilant, constantly working at it, constantly trying to make that weak armor strong, because the moment you forget about it, the enemy will take advantage and break it completely and bring you down.

So, to build that armor up strong and fast before it completely falls apart and you completely stop praying, you need to work at it constantly, <u>keep trying to improve your prayer</u>. If you pray three times, keep working every single day to make it five; if you pray late, keep working every day to pray early; if you are praying poorly, keep working on having humility in your prayer.

monument, like a mountain, each one incredible, powerful! Protecting you, guarding, and empowering you all the time.

Everything else in your life is dependent on how good your Salah is. Make your Salah excellent and everything else will automatically fall into place.

I pray but I still do sins.

<u>Salah WILL change you</u>. It will protect you. If you find that you are still doing some horrible sins, but you are praying with your heart five times a day, then know for sure your prayer will win over your sins. It will protect you. You will leave the sins, as long as you don't leave your prayer.

We also need to make sure that our prayer is strong, it's not empty of humility, for it to have the power to stop the major sins.

Here is a tip for you to build strong armor.

Keep track of your prayers, so you don't forget about them. Monday, Tuesday, Wednesday, Thursday, Friday, Saturday, Sunday. Make a chart with 7 columns and 5 rows. Write the days in the columns and prayers in the rows. Then score yourself every day. 10 out of 10, I prayed fajr on time and I was so good at my fajr, concentrated the whole time. 10 out of 10.

Maybe you were not so good. You prayed late. You only prayed after mom called you like 10 times, so it wasn't that great. Or you didn't wake up. So, you mark yourself 0, 1...

	Mon	Tue	Wed	Thur	Fri	Sat	Sun
Fajr	On time Humility -6/10						
Dhuhr							
ASR							
Maghrib							
Isha							

Or you can grade yourself, give yourself an A or D. But keep track of it. If you forget about it, the devil will take you down.

The things we keep track of and measure generally get better in life; when we forget about them is when they start getting worse.

Moreover, we need to constantly keep working at improving our prayer. Nothing in life stays the same, things are either growing or dying. Just look at anything, plants, machines rot, stars grow and die, clothes become dirty, rip if not maintained: it's either been growing or dying, getting better or getting worse. Nothing will just stay in the same state all the time. Your Salah is either getting worse or getting better.

If you are not actively trying to make it better, then chances are it's already getting worse. That means your armor has already started to become even weaker.

If not maintained even the most expensive airplanes start to rot.

We must constantly keep working on our armor, keep maintaining it, do any repairs if needed, shine it, polish it. We need to strengthen it constantly.

Gratitude

Having a grateful heart is the goal of a Muslim. Gratitude is your shield from sadness. It is hidden power behind sincere actions, which are done in gratitude to our Creator. Even when he is tired or scared or lazy, he does the good deed because he is grateful to his Master. It is what makes a Muslim almost invincible. No matter what happens, it doesn't destroy his/her happiness, his calm, because he/she is grateful. Gratitude is the healing for your heart. The happiness of our life is reliant on our gratitude.

> "How amazing is the affair of the believer. There is good for him in everything and that is for no one but the believer. If good times come his way, he expresses

Even science tells us today that the people who live the longest or happiest lives are the ones who are most grateful.

Allah (swt) has promised us that the more we thank Him, the more He will give us.

$$\text{وَإِذْ تَأَذَّنَ رَبُّكُمْ لَئِن شَكَرْتُمْ لَأَزِيدَنَّكُمْ ۖ وَلَئِن كَفَرْتُمْ إِنَّ عَذَابِي لَشَدِيدٌ ۝}$$

And (remember) when your Lord proclaimed: "If you give thanks, I will give you more (of My Blessings), but if you are thankless, indeed! My Punishment is severe." Quran 14:7

Is this promise because He needs your thanks? No, it is so you increase in your thanks. So you can appreciate what you have, use it for good out of gratitude to Allah not for sinning. Then Allah is going to grant you even more! The promise is not for the benefit of Allah. It is for your own benefit.

How grateful are you to Allah (swt)? How much do you remember to thank Him?

Do you think a person who doesn't even come to prayer is grateful to Allah (swt)?

What are they busy with, what has made them so lazy, that they can't come to prayer?

Are they too busy enjoying the blessings of Allah (swt) that they can't even come to thank the one who has given them these gifts?

In Surah Adiyat, Allah (swt) talks about war horses. He describes how fast the war horses are running, dust clouds forming from their feet thumping against the ground with force, sparks forming from their feet rubbing again and again against the ground.

What are they running towards? Danger! Enemy!

Even though they know it's dangerous and they can see the danger, they are still running towards it.

Animals can sense danger, they have a strong survival instinct. When they sense danger, they try to run away from it, or hide or try to protect themselves.

However here, the war horse is running towards it.

Why?

Because its master commanded it to. It's rushing towards danger on the command of its master.

As soon as the master says GO, the horse rushes towards danger. It doesn't go slowly; it runs fast, so fast that sparks form from its feet.

It doesn't pause, and think "Ahh, do I have to?" "Can I go later?"

It doesn't turn back. It obeys its master immediately and rushes on his command. Why?

Because it is grateful to its master.

What has the war horse's master given it? Food, water, shelter, little care, etc.

Who is your Master? – Allah (swt)

How much has your Master given you?

Far, far, far more…

How grateful are you to your Master?

How do you react when Allah (swt) calls u?

When does your Master call?

At least five times a day Allah (swt) calls us, calls us to a meeting with Him, a private meeting with Him. Salah!

How do you respond? Are you rushing to it?

Or are you like "Oh, I'll go in a few minutes." "Do I have to?"

Which one are you? Are you like a war horse, or slow like a snail? (At least the snail has an excuse for being slow, it's doing its best, what about you?)

The more you are grateful to Allah (swt), the faster you'd rush to your Salah, to meet Allah (swt). He calls you to the meeting and you go, you rush to meet Him, to thank Him.

The more you love Him, the more you will rush to Him.

Do you want to know how much Allah (swt) loves you? Look at how much you love Him.

If you want to know how much you love Allah (swt), then look at your prayer. How is your prayer? How much do you love your prayer? This is how much you love Allah (swt).

If you want to know how strong is your emaan? Then look at your prayer. How is your prayer? This is how strong your emaan is.

You know where the war horse is before the war starts. It's already there in the battle lines, lined up. It's not sleeping in the stable.

It is ready.

The same way, before the Salah begins, we should be ready. If Dhuhr is at 1 PM, you should be ready with your wudu. Ready to go meet the Lord of the world.

Allah (swt) swears by the war horses in the Quran and tells us that mankind is ungrateful to Him.

Rush to your Salah and show Allah (swt) how you are to Him. Rush to your prayer and show Allah (swt) how much you love Him. Be better than the war horses!

Alhamdulillah, thank you, Allah, for allowing us and ordering us to do salah 5 times a day to show gratitude to Him. (Without have appreciated so many things in my life and would have been way less happy)

(BTW did you think about this, we should thank Allah for everything He has given you and then also thank Him for allowing you and teaching to thank Him! Infinity!)

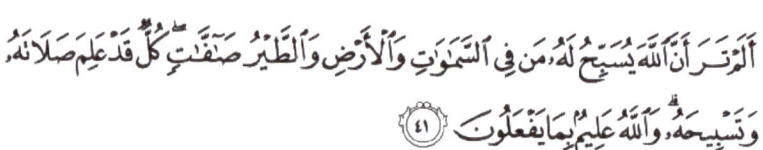

Do you not see that Allah is exalted by whoever is within the heavens and the Earth and [by] the birds with wings spread [in flight]? Each [of them] has known his [means of] prayer and exalting [Him], and Allah is knowing of what they do. (24:41)

Is Shaitan a Muslim?

Who is a Muslim? What would you say makes a person Muslim?

Generally, we would say somebody who believes in Allah (swt).

Does shaitan believe in Allah (swt)?

Yes, he does. Right?

He knows Allah (swt). He believes Allah (swt) is the Creator of all.

Allah (swt) is the one who created him. He knows that there are heaven and hell.

He knows that Prophet Muhammad (saws) is the Prophet of Allah (swt) and the Quran is the word of Allah (swt).

He knows all that. So, is shaitan a Muslim?

No, of course not.

Shaitan doesn't have any emaan. Shaitan is not a Muslim.

So that means you need something else to be a Muslim.

Shaitan is not a Muslim, because he does not obey Allah (swt). He disobeys Allah (swt).

He refuses to obey the command of Allah (swt).

He is not a Muslim because he does not submit to the will of Allah (swt).

One of the most important things Allah (swt) has ordered us to do is Salah. It is so important that Allah (swt) has commanded us to do it every single day, five times a day.

So what about somebody who refuses to obey this command of Allah?

Someone who says, "I don't want to pray 5 times, 2 times is enough for me."

I can't do Fajr, I will just do dhuhr or asr and that's it.

Or someone who says I am not going to pray five times as Allah has commanded. I will join them and pray them together once a day, just pray them all together at a time I want to pray.

Is this person a Muslim who refuses to pray as commanded?

You tell me. I don't know. Allah knows best.

But at least they are acting a little like shaitan. Right?

Allah (swt) ordered him to prostrate to Adam, who was better than him, but shaitan said, "No, I am not going to do it."

Allah (swt) has ordered us to prostrate to him five times today in Salah. When somebody says I don't want to do it, I'm too lazy to do it, this is too hard... is this not worse than what shaitan did?

He/she is refusing to prostrate to someone who is a lot greater than us — Allah (swt)

This is very serious.

Most of the Islamic scholars believe that this person is not a Muslim.

But Allah (swt) knows best. I'm not saying either way. Allah (swt) knows best whether they are Muslim or not. But you need to think about it.

This is a very serious matter.

If we are refusing to pray, we are at least a little shaitan. But we don't want to be anything like shaitan. We want to be like the greatest Prophet (saws), the greatest of the people whom Allah (swt) loves, InshaAllah.

So, we must try our best to do all our Salahs and on time and with our heart in it and be the exact opposite of the devil! Be among the best of the Muslims!

Salah Is a Pillar of Islam

Your Islam needs to stand on five pillars. The pillar of Salah is the one you build every day. If you didn't build this pillar, then would you be able to build emaan in your heart? If you destroyed this pillar, your entire Islam would be in danger of falling. The weaker this pillar is, the weaker is your emaan.

Build it strong and tall! Make your Salah strong and powerful!

Who Is a Hypocrite?

Allah (swt) has told us that the hypocrites are the people who will be in the deepest parts of the hell fire, where the fire is the hottest.

Hypocrites have always been among us. Even at the time of the Prophet Muhammad (saws), the hypocrites were present. They used to pretend to be Muslims, but in their hearts, they were not! They would say that they love the Prophet (pbuh), but behind his back, they would plot to kill him. They even used to come to the masjid to pray five times a day. Even the hypocrites pray, and Allah (swt) said that they would be in the deepest parts of the hell fire. Then what about someone who says, "I am a Muslim" and doesn't even pray?

Anyway, they used to come to prayer, but they didn't like it. They hated coming to prayer. They were only doing it to show off to people, to just get it over and done with. In their prayer, they didn't remember Allah (swt) much.

Can a Muslim turn into a hypocrite?

Yes, of course.

We are the ones saying that "we are Muslims" and, if we don't act according to it, we would be liars, hypocrites.

Think of hypocrisy as a disease that anyone can catch. If you are not careful, you will get this disease. We all need to protect ourselves from this poisonous, dangerous disease that can lead us to the deepest part of the hell fire.

This is shaitan's goal for you.

Your goal is to go to heaven, and you're not even thinking about it all the time.

Shaitan is thinking about his goal all the time. He has a goal and a plan for you. His goal is for you to be a hypocrite; that's his ultimate goal. So that you are in the deepest part of the hell fire, suffering the worst punishment. Shaitan

works his plan in steps, small steps which lead to his big plans. He builds one on top of another, kind of like Legos. Just like in Legos, you place brick on brick to build something big, right? That's how he works. Small steps, small sins, small evils; then major sins. Thus, he builds a great evil person. He's going to try to take you there. Step by step, he will try to build the qualities of a hypocrite in you.

But remember: you are stronger than him, especially if you are praying. Allah (swt) is also with you!

Allah has already given us what are the steps and what are the bricks he's going to try to build in you. Here are some of the clues for you.

$$\text{إِنَّ ٱلْمُنَٰفِقِينَ يُخَٰدِعُونَ ٱللَّهَ وَهُوَ خَٰدِعُهُمْ وَإِذَا قَامُوٓا۟ إِلَى ٱلصَّلَوٰةِ قَامُوا۟ كُسَالَىٰ يُرَآءُونَ ٱلنَّاسَ وَلَا يَذْكُرُونَ ٱللَّهَ إِلَّا قَلِيلًا ﴿١٤٢﴾}$$

Indeed, the hypocrites [think to] deceive Allah, but He is deceiving them. And when they stand for prayer, they stand lazily, showing [themselves to] the people and not remembering Allah except a little. (4:142)

وَمَا مَنَعَهُمْ أَن تُقْبَلَ مِنْهُمْ نَفَقَـٰتُهُمْ إِلَّآ أَنَّهُمْ كَفَرُوا۟ بِٱللَّهِ وَبِرَسُولِهِۦ وَلَا يَأْتُونَ ٱلصَّلَوٰةَ إِلَّا وَهُمْ كُسَالَىٰ وَلَا يُنفِقُونَ إِلَّا وَهُمْ كَـٰرِهُونَ ۝

And what prevents their expenditures from being accepted from them but that they have disbelieved in Allah and in His Messenger and that they come not to prayer except while they are lazy and that they do not spend except while they are unwilling. 9:54

Every time they come to prayer, they are like "Do I have to pray again? Is it prayer time already? I'm so sleepy, I don't want to go to prayer." "I just want to pray quickly and get over with it." They don't want to pray. They only come because they want to show someone, so they would even lie if they could - "Okay I have prayed."

Every single time, they come in and stand up in prayer, they are lazy. They don't want to meet Allah (swt).

Also, Allah (swt) says that even when they pray they are not thinking about Allah (swt); their mind is totally somewhere else. They don't want to meet Allah (swt); they don't love Allah (swt).

I am sometimes lazy to pray. Does that mean I am a hypocrite?

NO! That's not what I am saying!

Do you think a hypocrite would be reading this book? Learning all this, to try to get better in their prayer? Would they ever even care to improve their prayer? NO!

If you know in your heart that you do feel that you wish you were better, you wish you could pray better, you could be closer to Allah (swt), then – Insha'Allah – you are not one of them at all.

Maybe you find it hard and are not able to do it, but you really want to. Then, Insha'Allah, you are not one of them.

A hypocrite would never care to be better or want to be better.

But... this, often being lazy to come to prayer, or praying without ever even thinking about Allah, is a warning sign.

Because shaitan wants you to be a hypocrite, and "being lazy for prayer" is one of the qualities he wants to build in you.

One by one, he will try to build in you all the qualities of hypocrites, so that he can achieve his ultimate goal of turning you into a hypocrite.

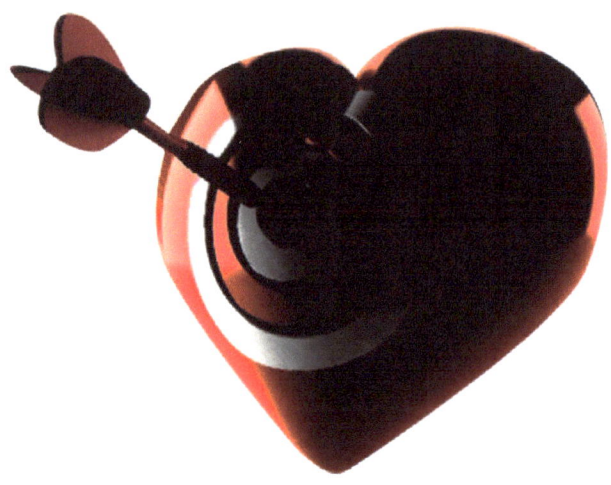

Just like you and your parents are trying to build the character of a great Muslim in you, similarly shaitan is trying to build the character of a hypocrite. The lazier you are for your prayers right now when you are 9, 10, 11, 12 years old, the easier it is for him to turn you into a hypocrite.

He is trying his best to train you to become a hypocrite. Every time you miss your prayer, or you delay it without reason, shaitan has succeeded over you a little more.

When the prayer time comes, then shaitan will come to you and make you delay it. "Wait, just 10 more minutes!" But you need to get up right away,

Get up, go and pray. If you don't go, if you say, "Let me just finish this, let me play a little more, let me play for just 15 minutes more," what are you saying? Do you know who you are saying that to? You are saying "Allah, wait just 10 more minutes, I'll come after I finish my game." Isn't that what you are actually doing? Saying, "Allah, wait 10 minutes, I am playing. I'll come later." That's pretty horrible, isn't it?

Do you want to have any qualities in common with the hypocrites?

NO!

Absolutely not. So, you say "I will not be like you. I will not follow you."

Hypocrites are lazy towards their prayer. I WILL BE THE EXACT OPPOSITE."

I WILL RUSH TO MY PRAYER LIKE THE WAR HORSES.

Hypocrites are the last ones to pray and I will be the first on

Beat everyone else in your home. Be the first one, the best one, the one who rushes to meet the Lord of the world.

This is just a picture of a trophy, but Insha'Allah you will receive the real great rewards from Allah (swt) in this life and next.

Close your eyes and imagine what it would be like to receive the real award and being honoured by Allah (swt) in the greatest assembly of all humans and angels on the day of judgment.

No matter what you were doing before prayer, leave it and go and pray.

What is more important to you than going to meet Allah (swt)? How can you delay your meeting with Allah (swt) for something else?

Is homework more important than Allah (swt)? Is a game more important than Allah (swt)?

When the prayer becomes due, then it becomes our number one priority to go and fulfill it as soon as we can.

Come to Prayer, Come to Success

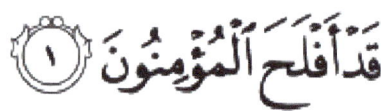

"*Successful indeed are the believers.*

Those who offer their Salaah (prayers) with all solemnity and full submissiveness."

[al-Mu'minoon 23:1-2]

Success lies in Salah. Each prayer comes with great blessings for you.

If you keep regularly putting something else before prayer, then that thing is never going to give you success. In fact, eventually, it is going to hurt you.

For example, let say a girl called Zega had a class at the time of Dhuhr. She had no time in her recess to do her prayer, because there were so many other things to do. She was always quite busy, with one thing after another during the whole school day. She wanted to pray but always felt, "Ahhh... I just wish I had more time."

Another girl, Aisha, on the other hand, also had the same amount of work. But, as soon as the recess bell rang, she would first go and pray.

So, she goes and prays, and then does her work.

Everything she does after her prayer has become a little easier for her. Somehow, she is now able to work twice as fast. The work that took her one hour before only takes ten minutes now!

How is this happening? Is it the blessings of the prayer? The angels helping her in every step? Removing all the obstacles from her path?

Yes! All this and more! The blessings of the prayer. It makes everything easier and filled with more blessings.

Her time is blessed, her work is blessed, her effort is blessed!

Every time you decide to delay prayer because you want to do something else, you are actually deciding to be worse at it, you are deciding to be less efficient at it. If you do the same thing after prayer, InshaAllah, it would be filled with much greater blessings and you would be far more efficient in doing it. So, think about it, was it really a good decision to delay your prayer? Did it really save you any time or help you in any work?

Think about it, has it ever happened to you that you were doing homework, then you went and prayed. When you came back, the homework had now become much easier! Alhamdulillah.

(You might even be playing a game and getting stuck. But when you go and pray – and pray WELL – you might come back and notice that you are doing so much better now!)

<u>Allah (swt) controls time.</u> He is the one who gives us knowledge. He is the one who controls everything and owns everything. Allah (swt) has the power to bless your time, so you can get done ten times more work in the same time. Allah (swt) is the best of providers.

When you come for Salah, putting Allah (swt) first, leaving all the other things, important things or just distractions, then remember: Allah (swt) will give you something way better in return.

وَيَرْزُقْهُ مِنْ حَيْثُ لَا يَحْتَسِبُ ۚ وَمَن يَتَوَكَّلْ عَلَى اللَّهِ فَهُوَ حَسْبُهُ ۚ إِنَّ اللَّهَ بَالِغُ أَمْرِهِ ۚ قَدْ جَعَلَ اللَّهُ لِكُلِّ شَيْءٍ قَدْرًا ﴿٣﴾

And whosoever fears Allah and keeps his duty to Him, He will make a way for him to get out (from every difficulty). (65:2)

And He will provide him from (sources) he never could imagine

And whoever relies upon Allah - then Allah is sufficient for him. Indeed, Allah will accomplish His purpose. Allah has already set for everything a [decreed] extent. (65:3)

Allah (swt) tells us that, if you keep your duty to Him, He will make a way out for you from every difficulty. He will provide for you in ways you could never even imagine!

That's right! At times, you might think there is no way, but Allah (swt) CAN MAKE A NEW WAY!

So why don't you turn to him when the time for prayer comes, instead of relying on those other things to provide for you or solve your problems?

Each prayer brings with it success. Don't miss out on that and be left behind!

Remember: Every time you decide to delay a prayer for no good reason or skip it to do something else, you are making a choice between Allah (swt) and that thing. You had a choice between this thing — game, friend, sleep, tv, book — or Allah (swt), and you have chosen to put this thing or person before Allah (swt). How incredibly unfair is this choice?

n another ayah, Allah (swt) says:

"Say that which Allah has is better than any amusement or merchandise! And Allah is the Best of providers." 62:11

Isn't it true?! All that Allah can give you is far greater than the things that are keeping you busy or entertained right now.

Whatever way you are seeking help, whatever it is you need help with, Allah is the best of providers. He can provide the greatest help to you.

> Every time we are choosing something else, we have to know that thing is going to hurt us in the end.

Alhamdulillah, for allowing us and teaching us to do salah 5 times a day and making it a way for our success. *(My life would be so much harder and I would be a total loser without it.)*

Nag Your Parents!

Do you get annoyed by your mom or dad, nagging you for prayer? Ya?!

So here is the solution to that:

Pray before your mom even gets a chance to ask you to pray. Do your wudu and be ready before she even thinks of coming and asking you.

You can surprise her! She will come to you and ask "Have you prayed? Come and pray," and you'll tell her "Mom, I have already done my Salah. I have prayed, have you prayed?" (Of course, you can only do this if you have prayed; otherwise, if someone lies, that is another extremely grave sin.)

You wake her up for fajr, instead of her waking you up. You'll be the first one, the best one in your house.

If you have prayed before everyone else, or if you are ready with your wudu to start Jamah before everyone else, then – of course! – you have the right to go about and remind everyone else. You can tell your siblings, younger or older than you, your parents, anyone! Be the first one and then you can nag everyone else.

وَأْمُرْ أَهْلَكَ بِالصَّلَوٰةِ وَاصْطَبِرْ عَلَيْهَا ۖ لَا نَسْـَٔلُكَ رِزْقًا ۖ نَّحْنُ نَرْزُقُكَ ۗ وَالْعَٰقِبَةُ لِلتَّقْوَىٰ ﴿١٣٢﴾

And enjoin prayer upon your family [and people] and be steadfast therein. We ask you not for provision; We provide for you, and the [best] outcome is for [those of] righteousness. *(20.132)*

Are You Praying for Your Parents or for Allah (swt)??

When I was younger, my mom would also nag me for prayer.

One day a thought came into my mind. Am I praying because I am afraid of my mom or am I praying because I love Allah (swt)?

Ariba have you done your salah?

If you only get up to pray after your parents have told you, nagged you, do you really know if you go to prayer because of them or because of Allah?

Ask yourself, are you praying only because you are afraid that mom and dad might scold you, or are you going because you love Allah (swt)?

Am I praying to show her or am I praying to be close to Allah?

Check yourself! Remember, hypocrites were only praying to show other people. We don't want to be anything like them. We shouldn't be praying ONLY to show someone else we prayed, even if it's our parents, but rather we only pray for the sake of Allah (swt).

Sure, your prayer will bring happiness and reward for your parents, but that's not the reason we pray, that's a benefit of your salah, not the reason for your salah.

So, if you really want to be sure that you are praying sincerely only for Allah, then you HAVE to become responsible for your own salah. Without anyone reminding you, nagging you, scolding you. You go to salah because you love to meet Allah, so you rush to it. Know the salah times and rush to your salah before anyone reminds you.

It is the job of you parents to remind you and it is your job to honour their request. So, you cannot say that don't nag me or not obey them when they tell you to pray. If you really want to make sure you are doing it for Allah, then you need to make sure you get ready before they get a chance to ask you!

وَإِذَا نَادَيْتُمْ إِلَى الصَّلَوٰةِ اتَّخَذُوهَا هُزُوًا وَلَعِبًا ذَٰلِكَ بِأَنَّهُمْ قَوْمٌ لَّا يَعْقِلُونَ ﴿٥٨﴾

And when you call to prayer, they take it in ridicule and amusement. That is because they are a people who do not use reason. (5:58)

Mom enjoys nagging??

Think about it, you find it hard to maintain just your own prayer. It's not easy! Do you think it's easy for your mom to maintain her own prayer and then ALSO maintain your prayer and the prayer of your siblings too??? How unfair is that?

Anyways, do you really still need your mommy to remind you it's prayer time?? Seriously??

Be responsible for your own prayer!

(If you want to learn more about why mothers nag and how to end it, then check out my Mother's Brain and Nagging Video. If you want to learn more secrets about mothers and develop a much stronger relationship with them, then check out the full program, My Guide to My Mother's Heart program.)

True Story: The Double-Edged Dagger

Omar (raa) was a really good man. A righteous man. One of the best friends of Prophet (saws). Allah (swt) loved him and he loved Allah (swt). Allah (swt) had promised him Paradise while he was still alive.

Prophet Muhammad (saws) said about Omar that, when Shaitan sees him coming down one way, he runs away to another road. Even Shaitan was afraid of his strong emaan.

Don't you wish you could have the emaan like Omar (raa)? Well, I am going to tell you in a minute how you can have that, Insha'Allah.

Omar (raa) was also a big man, really tall and strong. When he stood up, people thought he must be standing on something, he couldn't possibly be so tall. But he was!

People were also scared of messing with him because he was so strong.

After the Prophet Muhammad (saws) and Abu Bakr (raa) died, he became the Khalifa of the Muslims. He was the leader of the Muslims all over the world, in charge of all of the massive Muslim armies, a great leader, a just leader. Omar (raa) was known for his fairness and justice. He was also very kind and gentle, especially towards children and even animals. Even though he was a Khalifa, he would go out to do chores of old people.

The Muslims, especially the people of Medina, loved Omar (raa). He was dearer to them than even their own fathers, brothers, and sons.

One day a man decided to kill him. His name was Abu Lulu. Abu Lulu had got upset over something and, in his anger, he just wanted to kill Omar (raa).

But he was a small man. How was he going to kill Omar (raa)? So, he came up with a plan, an evil but clever plan. He took a dagger that was sharp at both ends and then he dipped the dagger into poison so that the poison stuck to the dagger. Then, he thought of a time when he could get close to Omar (raa) without Omar (raa) noticing.

What time could that be?

When Omar (raa) was praying, as Omar (raa) would be concentrating in his prayer, he would not notice him coming.

So, he went to the mosque at the time of Fajr Salah. He kept crossing rows after rows without anybody noticing him. Why? Because they were concentrating on their prayers.

He reached the front, right behind Omar (raa), who was the Imam, right in the front. He lifted his dagger, sharp at both ends, with poison stuck to it. He lifted and stabbed Omar (raa) in his back. He stabbed him and stabbed him, and then, as he was trying to run away, he stabbed seven other people.

IMAGINE THE SHOCK… THE PAIN…!

There was a large crowd praying behind Omar (raa). People in the back rows had no idea what was going on. Why had the prayer suddenly stopped? They didn't know that the man they loved so much had been stabbed.

Omar (raa) fell in extreme pain. But, as he was falling, even then he was concerned about everyone's prayer. He signaled to people so someone else would come and take his place, so the prayer could carry on.

Blood was gushing from his body, the poison was spreading in his bloodstream, getting to his heart. In extreme pain, he fainted…

What was going to happen now?

People loved him so much. They had already lost Prophet Muhammad (saws), they had lost Abu Bakr (raa), and now they were about to lose Omar (raa), the man they loved more than their families.

There was so much sadness in the city.

People were worried. "He is going to die! We need to wake him up to cure him. Wake up, Omar! Wake up, Omar!"

"Wake up, Omar. Wake up."

"Wake up, wake up."

"Wake up, wake up."

The medicine men, doctors came, trying different medications and tricks.

"Let's try this, let's try that." Nothing worked...

They kept trying and trying. "O, our leader, wake up."

"Wake up. Wake up."

They tried all sorts of treatments, but nothing was working. They just couldn't wake him up. What could they do?!

Finally, someone said, "I know how to wake him up."

"How?! Please tell us, how?!!"

He went and quietly whispered in Omar's (raa) ear...

"As Salah. As Salah."

Meaning, "It's time for prayer. It's time for prayer."

OMAR (RAA) JUMPED UP!

He jumped up and said, "It's time for prayer?! It's time for prayer?!"

He immediately woke up from just a whisper – "It's time for Salah."

Can you imagine how much he loved his prayer? How concerned he was for his prayer?

How important Salah was for him? How much he loved Allah (swt)? How much he loved his meeting with Allah (swt)?

Omar (raa) said, "There's no Islam for somebody who doesn't pray."

Now, what happens when you are sleeping?

Have you fainted? No, you're just sleeping.

What happens when the alarm goes bang bang.

Or mom/dad call you, "Wake up, wake up!"

Do you wake up with a whisper?

I hope from now on you will, InshaAllah. Maybe that's why Allah (swt) has bought the knowledge of this story to you, so you can be like Omar (raa).

I hope from now on, you will also wake up with a whisper, "As Salah."

This was the key to Omar's (raa) emaan and success. His prayer, his connection with Allah (swt). If you want to build emaan like that of Omar (raa), so that even the devil fears you, then you can! All you need to do is make the 10 minutes of prayer the most important thing in your life and the best 10 minutes of your day.

Omar (raa) was still in pain, blood was still gushing from his body, but he prayed. Then he died from that wound and poison.

So, tell me, is it okay to miss your prayer if you're really, tired or sleepy?

No.

What if someone is so sick they are dying, can they miss their prayer?

NO!

Ramadan only comes once a year, but if you are sick do you have to fast in Ramadan?

No, you don't need to.

Do you have to do Hajj if you are sick? No, you don't need to.

But Salah is different. We do it every day and, no matter how sick or weak we are, we are not permitted to miss this meeting.

Allah (swt) has allowed us easier ways to pray. For example: if someone can't stand up, they can pray sitting down on a chair or on the ground; if someone is so sick that they can't even sit, they can pray lying down; if someone can't move their body, they can just pray by moving their finger or even just their eyelids! Ya, that easy!

Even soldiers on the battlefield, when they're being attacked, even they have to pray. There is a different way that they pray, an easier way Allah (swt) has allowed for them, but they still need to pray.

So how can you say, "I'm so sleepy, I'm so tired. I can't pray."?

Allah (swt) doesn't want to make things hard for you. He wants to make things easy for you. He doesn't want to cause us hardship. That's why, out of His mercy, He has allowed all these easier ways.

But then why doesn't Allah (swt) allow us to just skip it if we are tired?

Hmm...this is like saying I really need to do homework, so let me skip lunch and dinner. Sure, you can skip a meal or two. You are not going to die. But will you be able to do your homework well? Of course not! Food is your basic human need. You need food to power up yourself.

Similarly, when we are sick or weak, we need rest, but most of all we need Allah's (swt) help. He is the one who can cure us. We are miserable when we are sick, and we need the happiness, calm, peace that the prayer gives us.

Even when you are tired and it's time for prayer! Prayer is not some hard exercise that will be too hard for you, but rather prayer is the coolness, the calmness that will heal your body and soul and refresh you, re-energize you.

> The Prophet, Allah bless him and grant him peace, said:
>
> "The coolness of my eyes is in the prayer."

When the Prophet (pbuh) wanted Bilal (raa) to call the adhan so they could go and pray, he would say "O Bilal, comfort us with it."

Similarly, every day of our life prayer brings peace, gives us inner strength that prayer gives to our soul, so we can be better human beings and say no to the temptations of doing sins our friends or shaitan are maybe inviting us to do.

Why Does Allah Want Me to Wake Up So Early?

Now, that is a very good question!

Let's see why might that be? What could be the possible answers?

Is it because Allah (swt) wants to torture you?

Is it because Allah (swt) wants to make it difficult for you to pray?

If Allah (swt) wanted things to be hard for us, wouldn't he make every prayer difficult for us? All we must do is get up and pray two rakat. That's all.

If Allah wanted to make it hard for us, He could have made it so that, instead of praying two rakat, we pray 30; instead of praying like we pray, we would have to go barefoot to the masjid, every day at fajr and then pray it and make sure you recite the entire Quran in every rakat. What if we had to wake up not once but five times in the night to pray? Sounds impossible?

Have a look at the picture below. People of a certain religion, go barefoot, crawl and even roll on the road, in the filth, mud, dust, bleed all the way to temples, to worship the idols.

Now, this is torture! This is something these people have imposed on their own selves and they gain nothing from it.

Allah (swt) doesn't want to make things hard for you, he wants ease for you.

Allah tells us in Surah Baqra, (meaning) "Allah intends for you ease and does not intend for you hardship"

Remember the prayer was meant to be 50, not five. Out of His mercy, Allah (swt) reduced it to five. This is who Allah (swt) is. He is not an angry God. He doesn't want to make things difficult for you. He wants to make things easy for you. He is not an unjust God. He is Ar Rahmaan.

> "When Allah created the creatures, He wrote in the Book, which is with Him over His Throne: "Verily, My Mercy prevailed over My Wrath." (Al-Bukhari)

Hmm... so the torture reason failed...what else could it be?

Is it because Allah (swt) enjoys the fact that you get up from sleep to pray to Him?

Does Allah (swt) get something out of it?

We have discussed this before. Allah (swt) doesn't need us. Whether you pray or not makes no difference whatsoever to Allah's (swt) glory.

He doesn't NEED you to give Him love, give Him praises, like Him or love Him. He doesn't need it at all. It is we who NEED that prayer.

So, if Allah has told us to wake up at dawn and do our salah, then that means - it is we who need to get up and pray at dawn. Just like you need food, air, love to survive and be healthy, you need Fajr, Dhuhr, Asr, Maghrib and Isha for your heart and mind to be healthy and for you to succeed in this life and next. You need these five and you need them at the times Allah told us to pray them.

It is Allah's (swt) favor to us that he taught us and allows us to do salah 5 times a day.

We are the ones who need to begin our day with Fajr at dawn, when angels are witnessing our prayer, starting our day with the meeting of Allah (swt) that will lift our entire day, fill it with protection and blessings, making everything easier.

Scholars of the past

We know of many scholars who were able to do 10 times more work during their day than we do today, they wrote hundreds of books in their life, taught people, did chores and so much more. They didn't have refrigerators, washing machines, cars, they had to walk long distances, wash their clothes with hands, they couldn't just search for anything or learn anything over the computer.

We have all that and more, so shouldn't we be doing many times more work than them?

But we don't. Most of the time, we just don't have time to do a few things we need to do or even meet our friends.

How is that?

Their days were powered up by the many more blessings, so they could do the same work that we do in half the time. Because they started the day by remembering the one who controls time, controls everything, who can solve any problem. They started their day by submitting themselves and all their problems and worries to Allah (swt).

Then, throughout the day, they remembered him and sought his blessings and these blessings increased their power in everything. They were able to do much more work than others, faster than others and far better than others.

They weren't as stressed as we get from too much work, because they were being sent salaam, peace from As-Salaam (As-Salaam is one of Allah's (swt) names. Allah (swt) is peace, pure, free of all evil).

Alhamdulillah, for allowing us to meet him in salah and teaching us such an easy way to worship him

Story Time

Space rocket, salah and a friendship

Esa had just moved into town. It was a brand new start and a brand new world. Esa's family had been unpacking for two whole days and had just got done. Esa was excited to be in a new place and eager to make new friends and have new adventures.

With a big breath, he helped to pick up the mattress and bring it to his room – the last task for the day. Now Esa could finally sleep and have a well-deserved rest.

But the peace was not to last.

When Esa awoke, he had to go to school. Esa was afraid; it was his first day and he was not familiar with the material being taught. Esa sat next to Harris. Esa and Harris got along quickly and soon they were playing together during breaks. Harris was eager for a new friend. He helped Esa catch up and explained the new homework to him.

Esa found the new work challenging. But, with the help of Harris, he was able to get through it.

Esa was concerned about where to pray. The first day, he was mortified and too afraid to pray at school. He thought to himself, "What will they think? Will I get bullied? Will someone hit me from behind? Will everyone laugh at me?" All these thoughts rushed through his head, and he was too afraid to pray.

When Esa returned home, he had tears in his eyes and his mother asked him what was wrong, wondering if his day had gone terribly.

Esa explained that he could not pray at his new school because he was too afraid of being different.

Esa's mom told him about the Prophet Muhammad (pbuh) and how he was also in a similar situation during the early days. He was the only Muslim praying at the Kaaba among many other people and the chiefs of the town, who were just like the students and teachers at school.

Esa's Mom said: "Can you imagine how different he must have felt? Moreover, people used to mock him, even hit him at times, but he never stopped praying. He would still go and observe his salaah at the Kaaba, despite all their mocking and threats.

"It must have been extremely hard for him, but he did it. And look today: he is the most beloved person to Allah (swt). Millions of people love him. Millions of people follow his footsteps and copy his every action.

"What if, many years ago, he had given up, thinking 'What will people think?'" or 'They will make fun of me today.' Would we even know Allah (swt) today? Would he be loved by millions of people today?

"He chose Allah (swt) above all. He put Allah (swt) first, and look how much Allah (swt) honored him both in this world and even more in the next. He didn't care about 'Will people like me or love me?' He cared more about 'Will

Allah (swt) love me?' And, today, Allah (swt) has made him loved by millions of people. He became the leader of not just the people, but even the Prophets!"

Esa said: "He was brave. I don't think I can do that."

Esa's Mom said: "What do you think made him so brave?"

Esa: "Allah (swt)?"

Mom: "Yes! His faith in Allah (swt). He was right there in the center of the city, doing his Salah, being the odd one out. But he knew Allah (swt) was with him. He was going to his meeting with Allah (swt), the All-Powerful. Imagine how strong and brave he must have felt! Next time, remember Allah (swt), and InshaAllah your heart will be brave like his too."

Esa was very inspired after hearing this story.

The next day, he marched to the principal's office and asked if the principal could help him pray because it was very important to him.

Esa didn't think that the principal would understand. The principal is very busy; he has to manage the whole school of hundreds of people. He was not a Muslim. Would he really understand?

However, the principal smiled, happy to see one of the pupils being strong in their faith and standing up for himself. He offered Esa his own office to use whenever he needed to pray.

Esa was surprised and energized by this gesture. He started praying all of his prayers in the principal's office, as well as praying extra Sunnah and Nafil.

Every day, walking back to his class, Esa felt stronger, more confident, more energized and happier. He felt as if angels were walking with him!

Esa runs away

Many days went by. Slowly, Esa settled in the new school. Things were going fine, but Esa was slowly becoming more and more lax and lazy in his salah.

The term was almost over and it was time for the final project. All the students had to pair up and present their project to the class.

Esa and Harris paired together naturally. However, Harris and Esa were both extremely nervous about standing up in front of the whole class and presenting their work.

They had done their work very well and they were torn. After weeks of work, they could fail their entire grade. Harris hyperventilated every time he thought about it, and Esa had to calm him down every time.

When the teacher asked the two to stand up and tell her when they would present their project, Esa's knees went so weak that he almost fell to the ground.

The two tried to think of a way to get out of it. Harris suggested that Esa should take on the presentation, so that Harris wouldn't have to speak. Esa explained that unfortunately he was equally – if not more – mortified at the thought of standing up and speaking to the whole class.

He asked the principal if he could be excused from delivering the presentation.

But, alas, there was no escape for the boys!

They determined to do it. With a big fake grin, they shook their pinky fingers and promised each other that they would both show up on the day and deliver their best.

It was Monday morning; the big day had arrived. Esa could feel his insides somersaulting. He walked to school, crippled with fear.

Just as he arrived at the classroom door, he saw the class had already gathered inside. This was the last straw for him; he couldn't stomach it any further. He gave in and ran away to the playground to hide.

As Esa sat in the playground crying, Harris was hiding in the basement of his house. Harris's mother finally forced him to walk to school. As Harris approached the school, he saw Esa crying in the playground.

He knew what had happened. So, he went to talk to Esa. Harris comforted Esa, and they shared their lunches. Ashamed of themselves, they found some respite from their embarrassment in their mutual kinship.

> What do you tink happened to Esa's bravery? Why is he acting so weak?

Half-an-hour later, the principal happened to be walking past and he saw the two. He became very angry with the boys for not being in their class, especially during their very important oral examination.

He brought the two back and gave them a harsh punishment in front of their entire class. On top of the initial stress of the oral presentation, the two were now officially being humiliated before their whole class and teacher.

The two were mortified and could not even look at each other after that. They both became very sad.

Rediscover the power

The next day, Esa went to the masjid. In a hazy mood, he droned through his prayers. After the Jumaat prayer had finished, he sat there for a while with an empty look on his face.

That's when the Imam, seeing Esa so sad, asked him if he knew about the power of praying regularly with humility and connecting with Allah (swt). Esa didn't reply, he just listened.

The Imam said that to pray with khushu, humility, is an opportunity to truly feel with your heart that you are in a meeting with Allah (swt). "Praise him the best way you can; you can tell Him all that is on your mind. Humble yourself in your meeting with Allah (swt), give Him all your worries, and ask Him directly for help."

Esa thought about what the Imam had said and, suddenly, he had a powerful purpose. He prayed with all his heart and mind, asking Allah (swt) to save him from the shaitan and help him in all his problems.

Before this salaah, Esa was an empty vessel, a field of sun-parched soil. But, after, it was as if the ocean of Allah's blessings suddenly sprang forth like the Zamzam well.

How perfect is Allah (swt)! Allah (swt) is the Master of the universe. The spring of the Zamzam well, which sprang from the desert, would have filled the entire Earth with water if Allah (swt) had not stopped it.

Just as He did for the mother of Ismail (pbuh), when we are most in need of Allah (swt) and we ask Him for help, He sends an unequivocal response.

It may not look like it, but everything had changed for Esa. Inside, he was a new person. He fought through his sadness and asked Allah (swt) with his heart in every salaah. He made a big effort towards Allah (swt).

Esa went to the principal the next day and he apologized. He still felt a lingering fear because of the anger of the principal.

But he knew that there is only one that should be feared, and it's not the principal; it's the All-Powerful – Allah (swt). The principal is still a slave of the Master of the universe.

In turn, the principal talked to him gently and explained to Esa that he had trusted Esa and had even offered him a place to pray in his office. But, when he saw what Esa had done, he had felt betrayed and disappointed.

Esa understood now and realized how the principal must have felt. He apologized profusely. The principal was delighted by Esa's forthcoming nature and his desire to improve.

He thought about Esa's grades and he offered to pass Esa and Harris because their work on the report for the presentation was good. They had scored only 49%, but he allowed the boys to pass the overall assessment because he saw how they had been punished enough and had learned a lot from their failures.

This was not to be the end, however. When Harris learned what had happened, he could not believe his good fortune!

> Alhadulillah! Allah saved him.
>
> Can you imagine how well Esa could have done if he had not laxed in his salah? The loss of Salah is indeed a great loss in every way.

Space, rockets and a broken friendship

The next term, Harris began to fool around in class. He became over-confident, believing he would get away with not doing the work.

Esa did not like the new change in Harris; thus, the two boys began to drift apart. While Esa realized the importance of hard work and the reality of

Allah's favor that had allowed him to pass, Harris foolishly believed he was the master of his own destiny and could get away with anything.

Worst of all, Esa was deserted by his best friend as Harris began to seek out the cool kids, pandering to them and wanting their approval.

Harris thought he was acquiring new friends. But, in reality, he was becoming even more isolated and a bit of a laughing stock.

The end-of-term oral presentation was again fast approaching, and Harris was woefully unprepared. He tried to get a partner, but everyone was already paired up with their friends. Even Esa was paired up and already working hard with his new partner.

One day, Harris was stressing out in the library, researching the topic he wanted to do, browsing the library for reusable rocket books.

When he saw Esa blissfully engrossed in a book, he asked him how he was doing. Esa replied, "Great! I'm doing a presentation on the future of space travel." Harris replied, "Really! I'm doing reusable rockets."

The duo reunified in their old friendship, talking about space rockets and space shuttles.

They both taught each other a lot in just that one hour of talking, and they both confessed to missing each other.

Harris confessed his woes – that he had not even found a partner and was struggling to finish his report on time.

Then Esa decided to share with Harris his experience of praying salaah regularly with khushu.

Esa shared with him how sad he had been before, that he had actually been feeling sick with his sadness, and how suddenly it had all changed when he'd starting praying with khushu.

Harris was bursting with excitement and wanted to know how to do it right away.

Esa, keen to do Dawah, spent hours with Harris, showing him how. It took them over five hours in a small private reading room, but Harris eventually learned to recite a prayer and how to pray with khushu. Esa gave Harris his favorite book on salah called "Discover the Power of Salah." 😊

Haris powers up

Harris went home, did the best wudu he could, and prayed with all his heart. Then he sat down to study. Usually, he would be distracted every few minutes, but this time he studied for the presentation for six hours. He only got up in between for his salah, which then again refreshed him.

When some topic was too hard for him and made him feel so weak that he couldn't go on, he would leave it to do after salah. Every prayer filled him with hope, confidence, and energy. Remembering Allah (swt) reminded him that Allah (swt) is Al Alim, the All-Knowing, the All-Powerful. He is always close, always responds to the prayer. Harris would then come back to studying, filled with so much strength and hope in Allah (swt) and ready to tackle any challenge!

His mother found him asleep on his computer desk after many hours of studying. She was proud of Harris. But Harris said: "It was nothing. I just cruised through this so easily." Harris was exhausted, though, and he asked his mother if he could take the day off, as he was extremely tired because he had barely slept the night before, except for an hour or two at his desk.

She allowed it, seeing he had really worked so hard and his eyes were tired from looking at the screen all night long.

Harris had completed about 95% of the work, but he still had to review the work he had done so far for spelling mistakes and other errors.

However, Harris had never had a whole day off school before, so he decided to sleep all day long. When he woke up at five o'clock, he just spent the rest of the day playing games and watching TV.

He forgot all about the presentation and skipped all his prayers. All the hard work he had done would soon come to an unpleasant end!

The next morning, Harris woke up late and it was almost time to go. He tried to correct some of the mistakes. But the more he tried to correct, the more he realized that huge parts of the presentation didn't make sense. And he had yet to properly connect the different parts of his work so that they all added up; currently, they were all jumbled up. Harris started to panic, but there was nothing he could do. Within moments, he was in front of the class presenting his work, and everyone saw the big mistakes he had made.

Harris was sure he would receive a bad grade and spent the lunch break alone under the stairs of the library, where no one could find him, scolding himself for ruining all his hard work.

He was just about to bang his head against the wall when Esa walked in. Harris explained everything to Esa, how he had almost completely finished the presentation, but had wasted time the next day watching TV and sleeping.

Esa explained that it was because he had not been praying that shaitan had got to him and made him lazy. That was the real cause of his problems.

Harris thought about it for a while, how things had suddenly changed for him when he was trying to work on his presentation and how praying had inspired him to work for hours. He had felt empowered knowing that Allah (swt) would help him, that the angels would surround him with blessings and shaitan would not be able to make him lazy.

Harris was very sad and lamented over how he could have done things differently and how everything was now lost.

Esa explained that all was not lost and that Allah always forgives those who repent and return to Him. He told Harris that, even though the presentation went badly, the true fate of all things is in the hands of Allah and He can change the result of anything, let alone his presentation.

Harris couldn't believe it, and he didn't. He told Esa it was impossible. "Our papers are graded; there's nothing that can be done now." He thought that maybe Esa was just trying to make him feel better. "But," thought Harris, "maybe there really is still a chance?"

Harris went home and couldn't stop thinking about what Esa had said and how he'd never really been wrong about this sort of thing before.

Harris was full of doubt, but he tried to pray. At first, he remained full of doubt, but slowly his desire to believe in the power of Allah (swt) grew.

His selfish obsession with his grades changed, and he instead began to believe in the greater scheme of Allah (swt), that He is the Almighty, that nothing happens without Allah (swt) knowing about it, and that He can change all things, just as He created them.

Harris prayed throughout the day and night, and he prayed with Esa in the principal's office too.

Harris had changed. He came to accept that, whatever happens, it is the will of Allah (swt), and all that he can do is be a good Muslim.

The day came in class a week later when the final grades were to be given. Harris had forgotten all about it. Instead of his grades, he was more focused on his faith, his deen. He was almost surprised when the teacher announced she would be reading the grades out.

Harris had long accepted that he would most likely fail due to his abysmal performance.

But, deep in his heart, there was a part of him that thought, somehow, Allah (swt) would save him.

The news arrived and Harris got a B-minus. He gasped and asked, "WHAT? I thought I would have failed for sure."

The teacher explained: "Don't be silly, Harris. Your knowledge about rockets and space was extremely detailed. You made a lot of silly errors, but you did well overall."

As Esa yelled in joy for his friend, Harris felt for a moment as if he was in a different world. It felt like history had written that he was going to fail, but he had shifted into a dream-world where he had passed with flying colors.

He knew now the power of Allah (swt) and the power of Salaah in helping us to stay connected with Allah (swt) and to succeed in life. He knew that he would certainly have failed had he continued on his previous path. Harris was certain that, if he was ever to leave his Salaah, he would return to his old ways.

And from that day forward, he never looked back.

O you who have believed, seek help through patience and prayer. Indeed, Allah is with the patient. (2:153)

What did you learn from this story? Reflect and write down your lessons.

Has something like this happened to you? Ask your parents or grandparents, has something like this happened to them?

What Is the Source of Your Confidence?

Make Allah (swt) a source of your confidence! Know that, if Allah (swt) is with you, then you are powerful.

As we humans are weak, we get distracted and we forget. You will forget how powerful Allah is and that, if He is with you, then you are so much stronger.

You will get weaker during the day, lose your power, your confidence.

But then Salah time will come and remind you again about Allah (swt)

Once again you will remember the power of Allah (swt), give Him all your worries and come back re-energized with confidence!

Your Report Card

Every day, at the time of Fajr and Asr, angels change shifts. At Fajr, the angels that are with you go back to Allah (swt) and new angels come down. Then at Asr, these angels go back to Allah (swt) and new angels come down.

When angels go back, they present their report to Allah (swt). Allah (swt) asks them, what was my slave doing? (Of course, Allah (swt) already knows!)

What were you doing at fajr or at asr? Praying? Sleeping? Playing games? Standing in prayer?

What would you want the answer to be for yourself?

أَقِمِ ٱلصَّلَوٰةَ لِدُلُوكِ ٱلشَّمْسِ إِلَىٰ غَسَقِ ٱلَّيْلِ وَقُرْءَانَ ٱلْفَجْرِ إِنَّ قُرْءَانَ ٱلْفَجْرِ كَانَ مَشْهُودًا ﴿٧٨﴾

Establish prayer at the decline of the sun [from its meridian] until the darkness of the night and [also] the Qur'an of dawn. Indeed, the recitation of dawn is ever witnessed. (17:78)

InshaAllah, wouldn't be wonderful if, every time they go back to Allah (swt), they report that you were in prayer - Fajr or Asr?

Wouldn't it be wonderful if, every time the angels leave you and new angels come to you, they meet you in the state of prayer?

Do You Want Shaitan to Urinate in Your Ear?

Prophet Muhammad (saws) told us that, when we don't wake up for fajr, that means that Shaitaan has peed in your ear. Yep! Disgusting, right?

You might not see it, just like you don't see the devil, but it's there and all the harmful effects of it are also there.

What do you think the devil was feeling when he was in your ear?

He was probably mocking you. Thinking what a loser you are. If you had just woken up, you could have been stronger than him throughout the day, but now he is peeing in your ear. This is his way of humiliating you.

So, if you don't want the pee of the devil inside you like that, wake up for fajr!

Remember that, when you are asleep at fajr (maybe even snoring), Allah (swt) is still watching you, waiting for you to wake up and come to the meeting with Him, get your sins forgiven, get your duas answered, fill your day with blessings.

Allah (swt) is watching and waiting for you, to shower you with His blessings...

Will you get up and take them?

How do you wake up for fajr?

Don't be like "Yawwn... I'm so slowly waking up." No!

Do you know how the Prophet used to wake up for fajr?

He would jump off the bed.

Jump off! Don't give Shaitaan time to put you back to sleep while you are slowly waking up and snoozing the alarm. Just jump off!

You can also say Audhubillah: "O Allah, protect me from the Shaitaan!" loudly, when you wake up.

You might wake up the whole house – doesn't matter. It's fajr; they should be up, lol.

> Narrated Abu Huraira Allah's Apostle said, "Shaitaan puts three knots at the back of the head of any of you if he is asleep. On every knot he reads and exhales the following words, 'The night is long, so stay asleep.' When one wakes up and remembers Allah, one knot is undone; and when one performs wudu, the second knot is undone, and when one prays the third knot is undone and one gets up energetic with a good heart in the morning; otherwise one gets up lazy and with a mischievous heart." (Bukhari)

For some people, it's really easy to wake up early at dawn. They would get up really early even if they were not praying, they were not Muslims. Other people have, Masha Allah, worked hard to build this habit over the years, so now waking up for Fajr is easy for them.

But if it's not easy for you right now, then remember the following.

Waking up for Fajr is also a beautiful proof of your love for Allah (swt). We all love sleep, we love it sooooooooo much. (Well, at least I love it soooooooooooooooooo much)

It's extremely hard to give it up and wake.

But you do, even though you love your sleep. You leave it, wake up, eyes half closed, banging into the walls at times, pour water over yourself, and come to the meeting with the one you love the most, your Rabb, Allah (swt).

You would probably not wake up that early every single day for anything else, but you do for your meeting with Allah (swt).

How wonderful is that love?

You wake up to meet and talk to the One you love the most.

Your love for Allah (swt) wakes you up at dawn and stands you up in prayer.

This act is proof of your love for Allah (swt).

Do you think you will show Allah (swt) your love every day, and Allah (swt) will do nothing in return?

Obviously not!

Allah (swt) will shower His love on you!

Allah (swt) is Al Wadud. The most loving. Allah's (swt) love is far more intense than you can ever imagine. Allah's (swt) love is incredibly greater than His mercy. Allah's (swt) love is for the select few people in this world.

What is it like to be the person loved by Allah (swt), the Lord of the worlds, the most merciful, the Owner of all?

What would it be like to enter your school as a person who is loved by the greatest Protector, the most powerful One?

What would it be like to wake up on the day of judgment as the person who is loved by the Master of that day?

How much will the heaven itself love you? How much will the angels love you? How much will the people with good hearts love you? In this life and the next…

Show Allah (swt) your love and Allah (swt) will show you His love!

When Allah (swt) loves a person, He calls Jibreel (pbuh) and says: 'I love So and so, so love him.' So Jibreel (pbuh) loves him, then he calls out to the people of heaven, 'Allah loves So and so, so all of you love him.'

So, all the angels and the people of heaven love him, and he finds acceptance and love on earth among good people.

If Allah (swt) hates a person, He calls Jibreel (pbuh) and says: 'I hate So and so, so hate him.' So Jibreel (pbuh) hates him, then he calls out to the people of heaven: 'Allah hates So and so, so hate him.' So they hate him and he is hated on earth."

Close your eyes for a minute and dream about this moment. Imagine what would it be like when Allah calls angel Jibreel and says your name announces to him that he loves YOU and then, Jibreel (pbuh) announces to everyone that Allah loves you

Prayer gives us an opportunity to remember and praise Allah (swt).

Of course, we don't praise Him because He needs it, but rather because Allah (swt) is praiseworthy!

Allah (swt) deserves all the praise and we must do our best to praise Him as best as we can.

It gives us an opportunity to express our awe and our love for Allah (swt).

How beautiful is it, when you stand up and use the best from the best of the words to praise the one you love the most – Allah (swt). ♥

Saying those same words of praise again and again, every day, makes them solid in our brains. Strengthens our belief in those words. Removing any doubt from it.

Moreover, praising Allah (swt) empowers us. It helps us. It reminds our own selves about Allah (swt), His attributes and who Allah (swt) is, so we can be stronger in emaan and belief in Allah (swt) and His attributes.

Alhamdulillah, for allowing us to praise him in salah 5 times a day and teaching us the best way to do it. *(Without it I would surely not have praised Allah on many days)*

First Check on the Day of Judgment

إِنَّ ٱلَّذِينَ ءَامَنُوا۟ وَعَمِلُوا۟ ٱلصَّٰلِحَٰتِ وَأَقَامُوا۟ ٱلصَّلَوٰةَ وَءَاتَوُا۟ ٱلزَّكَوٰةَ لَهُمْ أَجْرُهُمْ عِندَ رَبِّهِمْ وَلَا خَوْفٌ عَلَيْهِمْ وَلَا هُمْ يَحْزَنُونَ ﴿٢٧٧﴾

Indeed, those who believe and do righteous deeds and establish prayer and give zakah will have their reward with their Lord, and there will be no fear concerning them, nor will they grieve. (2:277)

The first thing that will be asked on the day of judgment is: How was your prayer?

The first thing angels will check is: How was your prayer? If your prayer was not good, then you are in the DANGER ZONE, no matter what other good deeds you have done.

Someone might say, "Oh, but I gave a million dollars in charity." Doesn't matter!

The angels know that, if his Salah was not good, then, of course, he has many other major sins. His armor was weak, he didn't check himself every few hours. Shaitaan must have trapped him in great sins. He didn't wash his sins with wudu and Salah every day.

So, of course, his bad deeds are immense.

On the other hand, there might be you, whose prayers were great. All on time, good quality prayers, prayed with humility. The angels will immediately put you in the SAFE ZONE. You will not be questioned hard. You might think –

Umm... I know I had some sins. I had a lot of them. I did some bad things.

But the angels will tell you not to worry because your armor was strong, you were checking yourself, Shaitaan couldn't trap you in his big plans, in major sins. Plus, because you were praying all the time, your minor sins were being washed off every day!

You are safe! Your Salah has saved you!

People who won't be able to bow down

On the day of judgment, at one point all of creation will bow down to Allah (swt). All except some people. The people who refused to bow down to Allah (swt) in this world, refused to pray, Allah (swt) will not let them bow down to Him on the day of judgment. They will try to bend their backs then, but they won't be able to.

How would a person feel then? All of creation is bowing down, and they are exposed for what they used to do. Allah (swt) will not let them bow down.

Where Will You Be Standing?

On the day of judgment, people will be standing according to their Salah. Those who prayed, prayed on time, prayed good quality prayer with humility, they will be closest to Allah (swt) and, Insha'Allah, under the shade of the throne of Allah (swt).

But the people who didn't pray at all, who refused to pray, knowing that Allah (swt) is the one they should bow down to, they will be standing furthest away from Allah (swt), they will be standing near people like Firaun, the evilest human beings.

Where do you want to stand? Today, the choice is yours, on the day of judgment you won't have a say in it!

League of Musallin (Those Who Pray)

People in heaven will be so happy, they are so happy! They have entered heaven! Insha'Allah, when you enter heaven, you will be amazed. People will be amazed at how much reward Allah has given them for the smallest of good deeds. Maybe you might say "Wow, this whole mountain of chocolate, these palaces of pearls, these rivers of honey are all for me! Allah (swt) has given me all this just because I shared my pencil? Or this is the reward of praying just two rakat of fajr! WOW!

"I had no idea I would be getting so much reward for even the smallest of good deeds! This is beyond my farthest imagination. Allah appreciated me so much?!!"

"Oh, but what about my sins... I know I had many sins."

But, you know what? Allah (swt) forgave them. He erased many of your sins.

They're not even in your record anymore. Allah (swt) forgave you.

Allah is so extremely merciful, loving and forgiving. He doesn't just forgive...

Let me tell you a wonderful story that Prophet Muhammad (saws) told us to show us how much Allah (swt) loves to forgive.....

Story of the Lost Camel

Once there was a man traveling all alone in a desert with all his belongings, food, and water on a camel. He stopped at one point to rest and went to sleep. When he woke up, he was shocked! The camel was gone with all his water and food!!

He was terrified; he searched and searched and searched. He looked everywhere. He was left all alone in the middle of the hot desert without a ride, food, or water. He had no chance of surviving. How could he travel on foot in the wide hot dry desert, and that too without water and food?

He looked and looked, he was extremely sad, the camel was lost... this man was going to die....

Then suddenly he turned around and the camel was right there!

With all his food and water!!!

He was so happy, so happy, soooooooo very happy.

He said, "Ya Allah, you are my servant and I am your slave."

Hmmm... sounds wrong? No, it's not a typo!

He said, "Ya Allah, you are my servant and I am your slave"

He was SOOO extremely happy that he didn't even know what he was saying in his happiness. He mixed up his words.

Can you imagine his happiness? Now comes the incredible part...

The Prophet Muhammad(pbuh) told us that Allah (swt) is happier than this man when you repent from your sin, when you leave your sin and seek forgiveness and return to Allah (swt).

Incredible, isn't it?! Allah (swt) doesn't need you. It makes no difference to the glory of Allah (swt) whether we are in heaven or hell. Yet, He is so loving, so merciful to you, He cares so much about you, that when you leave the sin and seek forgiveness, not only does He forgive you but He loves you even more!

You think you are happy when Allah (swt) forgives you! Allah (swt) is many times happier when He forgives you. No wonder He has made all these easy ways for us to seek forgiveness, such as salah, which washes away your sins like a bath, or like wudu. With every drop of wudu, your sins are washed away.

Could it be any easier to seek forgiveness?

Now, let's go back to what I was telling you about the people entering heaven and being amazed. People of heaven are now finally seeing the reality of the incredible love and mercy of Allah (swt).

But then they see the people in hell fire.

Their bodies burning, flesh burning, their skin's burning. They're drinking boiling water, eating puss from wounds; their skin is being ripped from their body.

It's terrible!

People in heaven have just seen how forgiving and full of mercy is Allah (swt). How much Allah (swt) has forgiven them and multiplied the reward of every good deed.

They are shocked! How could anyone enter hell fire when Allah (swt) is so full of mercy, so forgiving? What did they do to end up there? So, they ask the people of hell, "What did you do?! How did you end up here?!"

Then the people of hellfire answer and they give a long list of answers. But the number one reason on their long list is:

We did not pray. We are here because we didn't pray!

They will say, "We were not of those who prayed," Verse (74:43)

They were not in the league of Musallin.

You know now, after learning all that you have learned, you know exactly why that is. They were not checking themselves, they were not stopping at pit stops, shaitan took them down the wrong road, they didn't wash their sins, their sins kept making their hearts darker and darker, and it kept becoming easier for them to do bad deeds. They did not have strong armor, so of course the devil trapped them, so of course they have a long list of major sins.

If only they had maintained their Salah, they could have been in heaven, forever in peace, loved by Al Waduud, the most loving one, Allah (swt).

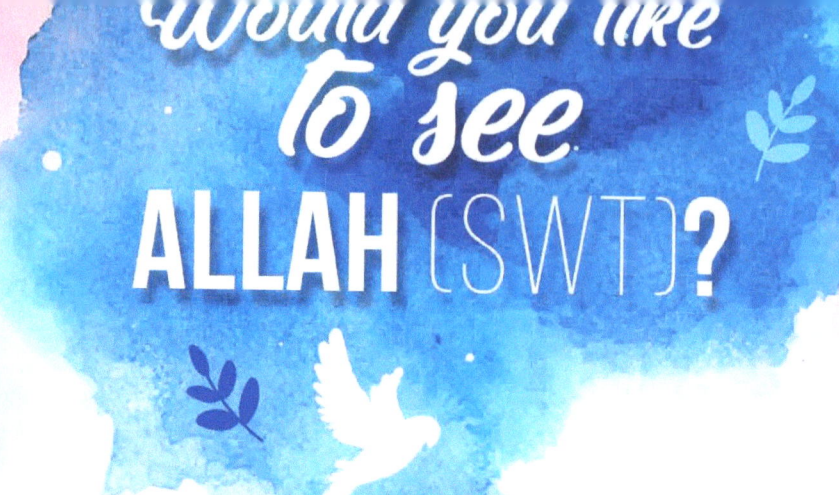

Would you like to see ALLAH (SWT)?

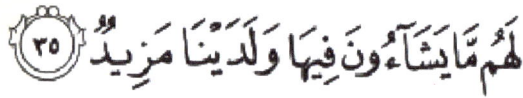

"There they will have all that they desire, and We have more (for them, i.e. a glance at the All-Mighty, All-Majestic)" [Qaaf 50:35]).

The Prophet Muhammad (pbuh) once said that Jibreel came to him with something like a white mirror in his hand, on which there was a black spot.

The Prophet Muhammad (pbuh) said: 'What is this, O Jibreel?'

Angel Jibreel said: 'This is Jumu'ah (Friday); it is the master of days and we call it Yawm al-Mazeed (the day of more)'

The Prophet Muhammad (pbuh) said: 'O Jibreel, what does "more" mean?'

Angel Jibreel then explained to him what "more" will be there on Yawm al-Mazeed:

Jibreel said 'Allah (swt) has allocated a valley in Paradise that is more fragrant than white musk.

When Friday comes, Allah (swt), will descend from His Throne ('Arsh) to His Kursiy, and the Kursiy will be surrounded with seats of light on which the Prophets will sit.

These seats will be surrounded with footstools of gold on which the martyrs will sit.

All other people will come down from their chambers and sit on fragrant sand hills.

Those who sit on the sand hills will not think that those who sit on the footstools and seats are any better off than them. *(Meaning no one will be jealous or even feel bad for being on lesser seats.)*

Then,

Allah, Owner of Majesty and Honor will appear and say:

'Ask me for anything.'

People will say: "Be pleased with us, O Lord."

Allah (swt) will say: 'It is because I am pleased with you that you are in My Paradise, and you are honored.'

Then,

Allah will say (again): 'Ask me for anything.'

They will say all together: 'We want you to be pleased with us, O Lord.'

Allah will ask them to testify (take an oath) that He is pleased with them.

Then Allah will say again 'Ask me for anything.'

And then they will ask of Allah (swt) for things until each one of them is finished. They have got everything they could ever ask for.

But Allah wants to give them even more on this great day.

Then, Allah will grant them that which no eye has seen, no ear has heard, and it has not crossed the mind of any human.

Allah (swt) will lift his veil and they will be able to see the face of Allah (swt).

The sight of the face of Allah will be dearer to them than anything else in Jannah. Everything in heaven, all the joy and happiness will be nothing compared to the happiness of seeing the face of Allah (swt)

Will you be there on this Friday? How close will you be sitting to Allah (swt)?

What will it be like to see Allah (swt) smile at you?

What will it be like to talk to Allah (swt), when He is pleased with you?

Will you be on the golden stools or the sand hills?

What will you say? What will Allah (swt) say to you?

Will He talk to you about your meetings with Him in prayers?

What will it be like to have a meeting with Allah (swt) in heaven when you can finally see His face?

Finally, being able to see the face of Allah (swt) is the greatest happiness a human being can ever experience.

This is the ultimate goal of our life.

Being deprived of and not being able see the face of Allah (swt) will the greatest punishment for the people of hell fire. Do you think Allah (swt) will show Himself to the people who didn't want to come to meet Him in Salah? Do you think He will show himself to the people who were lazy to meet Him in this world?

﴿حَافِظُوا۟ عَلَى ٱلصَّلَوَٰتِ وَٱلصَّلَوٰةِ ٱلْوُسْطَىٰ وَقُومُوا۟ لِلَّهِ قَٰنِتِينَ﴾

Maintain with care the [obligatory] prayers and [in particular] the middle prayer and stand before Allah, devoutly obedient. (2:238)

Prophet Muhammad (pbuh) once told the people that we will see Allah (swt) as clearly and easily as we see the moon in the sky. Just like you don't need glasses to see the moon. You don't need to line up to see the moon. It is clear and bright right there. Then he said, so make sure you don't miss the fajr and the asr prayers. That means there is a direct link between your fajr and asr and your ability to see Allah (swt) in heaven.

Alhamdulillah that Allah (swt) has allowed us to meet him in salah in this world and earn our place in Paradise through it.

I am so excited for this day.

May Allah (swt) make you and me all the people who read this book and our families, from the people who will one day see His face in Jannah.

Ameen

Insha'Allah maybe you and I will also meet in Jannah on that day and have a big party!!

Do You Have a Time Machine?

If you prayed right on time or you prayed at the end of the time, do you think the reward will be equal?

No, the later you are praying, the lesser your reward is. This is a reward that you can never get back; well, not unless you have a time machine.

The more you are delaying your prayer, the lesser will be the reward. What do you think Shaitaan wants you to get? 100% or 10% or 0?

He wants you to get negative!

He will keep making you delay your prayer so your reward is lesser and lesser, keep saying just wait 10 more minutes, there are three more hours, you can pray later – and keep reducing your reward.

But if you want to maximize your reward, then rush to your prayer immediately and get the maximum you can.

If you miss prayer, can you really make up for the reward you lost? Never, it's gone forever, you can't go back in time and pray that prayer.

Of course, if you didn't pray, you still must make up for the prayer, to save yourself from the sin of not praying. But the loss of the reward is something that can't be made up.

It will never ever come back!

> How much is the reward of any prayer?
>
> No one knows, because it's like infinity!
>
> The better is the quality of your prayer, the greater the reward will be inshaAllah.

Once a particular fardh salah of your life is gone, then it's gone...it will never come back.... it's an immense loss...

You can pray a lot of nafl, but that's just extra you are doing. Moreover, fardh is not like sunnah or nafl. The reward of a fardh is immensely greater than the reward of nafl.

Amazing isn't it, even though it is obligatory, even though it is something you need, Allah (swt) rewards you incredibly for doing it. Is there anyone in the entire universe who appreciates you more than Allah (swt)?]

There are so many, it's okay if we miss one.

> Prophet Muhammad(saws) said, losing one prayer is like losing your entire family.

Have you seen anyone who has lost their entire family? Maybe the refugees?

Have you seen their sadness?

When we miss the prayer, that is how great a loss we have had. We just don't realize it.

May Allah (swt) protect us, but that's how sad we might be on the day of judgment for the loss of each and every single prayer.

Even the people in Jannah would regret not praying just one more prayer. If the people of the graves could come back or could talk to you, they would tell you they would give up all of the enjoyment they had in their life just for two more rakat of prayer.

What is your number?

YOU have a specific number of prayers that you will get to pray.

An exact, specific number. There are only five fardh prayers in a day, and you can't just add one more.

There is a specific number of prayers that you will get to pray until the day you die. You have a limited number of prayers in your life. You will not get a single more fardh prayer than that number in your life.

What is your number? How many have you already lost?

If You Really Knew

Prophet Muhammad (saws) said, "*While a man was going on a way, he saw a thorny branch and removed it from the way and Allah became pleased by his action and forgave him for that.*"

The Prophet (saws) further said, "If the people knew the reward for pronouncing the Adhan and for standing in the first row (in the congregational prayer) and found no other way to get it except by drawing lots, they would do so, and if they knew the reward of offering the Zuhr prayer early (in its stated time), they would race for it and, if they knew the reward for 'isha' and fajr prayers in congregation, they would attend them even if they were to crawl."

The Prophet Muhammad (saws) tells us about a man who removed a thorny branch from the road, and Allah (swt) appreciated that so much that He forgave him!

We don't ever realize how merciful Allah (swt) is, how much he appreciates our smallest actions. Allah (swt) is Ash Shakir and Ash Shakur! He appreciates our actions even if they are as small as a smile, and He appreciates each action immensely.

Now, think about this: if Allah (swt) appreciates the small action of removing the branch so much, then how much does Allah (swt) appreciate you coming to Salah with sincerity every day?

Forget it, you can't... it will blow your mind! You can never understand how much Allah (swt) appreciates each and every one of your prayers. Think infinity times infinity!

That's why Prophet Muhammad (pbuh) said: "If the people knew the reward for pronouncing adhan they would do lucky draws for it."

Because there would be so many people eager to do it, they would have no choice but to draw lots.

Also, the Prophet Muhammad (pbuh) said, "If they knew the reward of offering Dhuhr early, they would race for it."

Not sit and delay, thinking, "There is still two hours before asr." They would race to it like war horses, to get the easy and immense reward.

"If they knew the reward for isha and fajr prayer in jamah, they would attend them even if they had to crawl to it."

How do you think you would feel on the day of judgment about KNOWING all that you have missed out on? How would it feel to KNOW the easy reward you could have earned but is lost now?

You are alive right now. You can stop yourself from losing all this reward. You know better now than to lose all this reward. So rush to your prayer from today and pray it with sincerity!

Praying at School

Most likely dhuhr is a few hours before you come back home. Ideally, you should do your best to pray at school but, if you absolutely can't, then pray as soon as you get back home.

"But.... I go to non-Islamic school."

"There are no Muslims in my school."

"I have no time to pray in school."

I have heard all of these and more… but now let me tell you two true stories from two of my students.

First of a boy in a public school in America called "Legs Shaking with Fear."

Legs Shaking with Fear

He had just joined a new school and was the only Muslim in his school. He wanted to pray dhuhr on time. So he went and talked to his teacher and his principal, told them that he is a Muslim and we need to pray five times a day. He asked the school to give him any place for 10 minutes to pray during the day.

The principal said, "That's fine, actually you can just pray in my office. I am mostly not even in my office during the day, so feel free to come in and pray here."

The principal's office had glass doors. That meant that everyone walking outside could see him. They would probably be wondering, what is this boy doing, kissing the floor in the principal's office?! You can imagine how awkward it would have been for him. What if his friends saw him? What would they think?

He told me that the first day he went in to pray, his legs were literally shaking with fear. He was terrified, worried about all the people watching him from outside.

Despite his fear, he continued, because regardless of what people think of him, he was more concerned about pleasing Allah (swt)

But then he said, "Now I go there every day. It's so easy... I go pray and come back. I don't even think about anyone watching me. I am not scared at all."

So, ya, at first it will be difficult. It might be scary, but you do it for the sake of Allah (swt) and, Insha'Allah, everything will become easier.

If you decide not to pray, then think about....

Why have you decided to not pray at school?

Because you are afraid of other people? Are they more important to you than Allah (swt)?

Are you more concerned about what they would think than you about your relationship with Allah (swt)?

Are you not putting these people before Allah (swt)?

Same goes for work, classes, games... whatever. Are these things more important to you than Allah (swt)?

If yes, then know that this is a minor shirk! We have put all of these things/people before our Lord.

No, I hope that is not the case. Maybe you just didn't think about it like that before and, InshaAllah, now you have and now you will try your best to do better.

Now the second story of a girl from Australia who prayed in the toilet.

She was so terrified of other people seeing her praying that she used to pray in the toilet!

Yep! The toilet!

I am sure you are thinking, she should not be praying in the toilet. You are right, we shouldn't pray in the toilet.

But before you judge her for praying in the toilet, look at her love for Allah (swt).

She is afraid of people seeing her, but she also loves Allah (swt) so much that she doesn't want to miss or even delay her meeting with Allah (swt). She could have just decided to not pray at school. But no; instead she decided to pray on time, even if it meant praying in secret in the toilet.

What made her do that? Her love for her Salah made her do it, her love for Allah made her do it.

And look now: Allah (swt) has made her an example for you and hundreds of others like you who read this book!

There are hundreds and thousands of children all over the world, going to schools where they might be either the only Muslim in the school or one of very few. But they are still praying at school, in store rooms, in drama rooms, libraries, empty classrooms, playgrounds, meeting rooms, auditoriums... These are just some I have heard of directly from children. They pray in recess, lunch time; sometimes they ask for permission to be 10 minutes late to class so they can pray.

Now you know that it's possible.

Think about what would you say to Allah (swt) if He asked you why did you pray late every day at school? What if He shows you all these hundreds of children, some in your own city maybe, who were praying at school?

Allah (swt) is your Rabb. This is the most important relationship of your life. Put Him before everything else!

Show your love for Allah (swt) and Allah (swt) will shower you with His love!

He will fill the hearts of the people with love for you.

All the people you maybe worried about that will make fun of you or not like you, Allah (swt) can fill all their hearts with love and respect for you

Make a Prayer Buddy

When you pray in Jamah, your reward multiplies 27 times or even more!

How many people do you need to pray in Jamah?

That's it, just two and your reward is now 27 times more!

Your dad, your mom, your sister, your brother, grandparents... anyone could be your prayer buddy.

Plus, when you have a prayer buddy, then – InshaAllah – you can help each other maintain your prayer. Keep encouraging each other. If one is slow, the other one can make sure they get up. Support each other in maintaining good prayer.

Build Your Soldiers

SUNNAH   NAFIL

If you only pray for fard/obligatory prayers, your fard is in danger! Because shaitan will keep attacking you, telling you to stop.

You need your soldiers. Your soldiers are your sunnah/nafl (extra) prayers. The more you are praying these extra prayers, the more protected will be your fard (obligatory) prayer.

Then the Devil first has to stop you from praying the extra ones, and only then can he stop you from fard.

SUNNAH

NAFIL

Ask Allah (swt) for Help

This, right now, is the help that you probably didn't even make dua for. Now, imagine if you made dua. How much more is Allah (swt) going to help you!

Allah (swt) has given you more of the knowledge, inspiration, to help you pray better. But if, after today, you pray the same way, if you are still lazy and are still delaying your prayer and you improve nothing in your prayer, what does that show? Would that be very grateful to Allah (swt)? No, it would be showing Allah (swt), "I really don't care. Even though you gave me this knowledge and I learned, I still don't care."

But no, you are not like that. You love Allah (swt) and want to be closer to Him. That's why you have invested all this time and read all of these pages.

InshaAllah, you are going to try to pray on time from today.

You don't need Mommy to remind you when it's prayer time.

You can take responsibility for your prayer. Find out the prayer times, write them down, set your alarms and be ready.

رَبِّ اجْعَلْنِي مُقِيمَ الصَّلَاةِ وَمِن ذُرِّيَّتِي ۚ رَبَّنَا وَتَقَبَّلْ دُعَاءِ ۞

My Lord, make me an establisher of prayer, and [many] from my descendants. Our Lord, and accept my supplication. 14:40

Khushu and Quality Of Salah

In this book we discussed the incredible power and the benefits we get from our salah. We discussed the power we get from praying on time and regularly

But did you know that salah also has a power source?

The more the salah is powered up the more it will power you up!

Khushu is the power source of your salah, it determines the reward you will get from your salah and how much your salah will benefit you

In the next book I will share with you some incredible true stories of khushu and some fun stories to help us connect with our salah

I will also give you some very simple and practical ways that you can use to make sure you have khushu in your salah

To make sure you get the next book visit

www.emaanpower.com/powerupsalah

What are people around the world saying about Emaan Power programs

"I really recommend this course for other children to learn about self-appreciation and leadership "

Nedaa (Mom of 12 yr old) , USA

It was really fun and interactive for me to interact with other people around the world and working together. My teacher (Ariba) is kind and acknowledge what we think during the lesson. I like the way she conducts the class.'

Iman, UK

My kids and others can benefit by learning how to take responsibility of their own learning. Showing them the practical skills required to prioritising their time, their daily connection with Allah through the Quran, excelling in everything they do such as study and getting involved in initiatives that benefit the community. Kids listen and absorb everything being said but developing their practical skills will help them apply the knowledge gained and hence be a long term benefit for them throughout their lives.

Rana Finj, Australia

"Alhumdolilah you are a great mentor for my kids. They love the way you teach and present. They Alhumdolilah talk to you informally, whatever question they have in mind, and you present the answer very well to their queries."

Farheen, UAE

In today's smart world, it's really challenging to involve our kids in a positive activity unless it's been designed in an interesting way. Kudos to Ariba for making this course really lively and exciting for my daughter who is not an easy to please child. She was thoroughly involved. I also liked the project, scrapbooks and community work that gave her real knowledge of the issues and how islam helps us handle these. Thus she was able to establish the link between the two. I would highly recommend this course to other kids. I really appreciate the effort and hard work of Ariba in a field that is totally ignored by muslim scholars. Well done and jazak Allah khair

Shuhair, USA

"This class bring the Islamic teaching into practice and help the child adopt Islamic believes and way of life without even trying or feeling "different" It inculcates the basic values of life in them and gave them a new respect for islam as the best way of life."

Swalehah Khouratty

"Definitely one of the best courses I have ever taken. The basic vocabulary, interactive live videos, sunnah competition and much more make this a fun and engaging course for kids of all ages."

Tarik, 13 yrs Old , Saudi Arabia

We have done a number of the Emaan Power courses and the boys have enjoyed all of them Alhamdulillah. The courses are interesting, relevant and fun. The courses provide kids the opportunity take on projects within their communities to benefit the ummah at large..

Sohret, Australia

Great experience, very engaging and opens up kids thinking process and problem solving. Very safe and friendly atmosphere. Appreciate your willingness to work with them without judging them yet letting them ask questions to open up their minds

Onaisa, Canada

Salah Video Series

Short inspirational engaging videos for your children, based on much of the content of this book.

To help your kids engage with the content of this book in a visual way.

You can play these as regular reminders on your device.

To find out more about this series visit

www.emaanpower.com/salahvideos

Emaan Power Live Courses

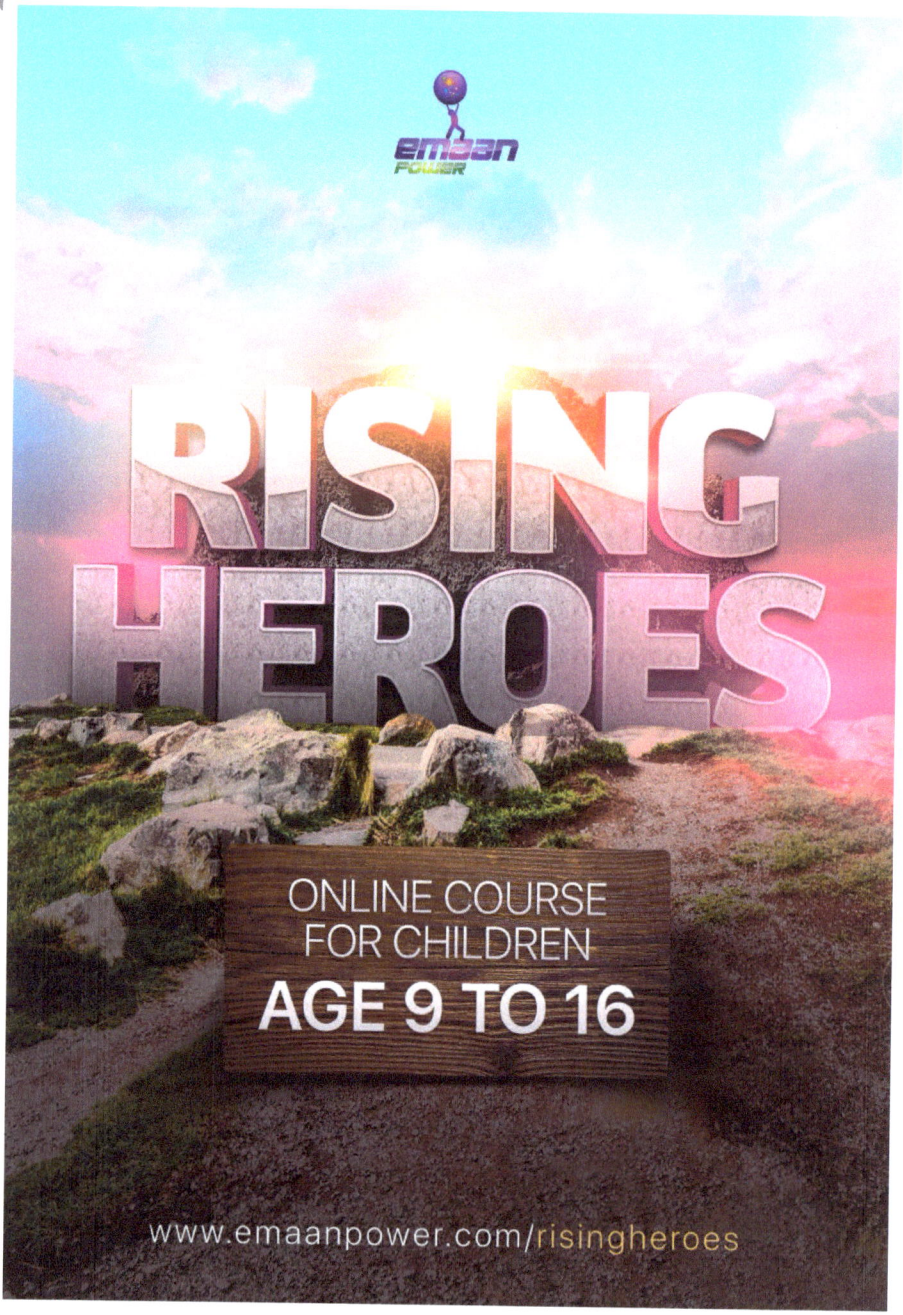

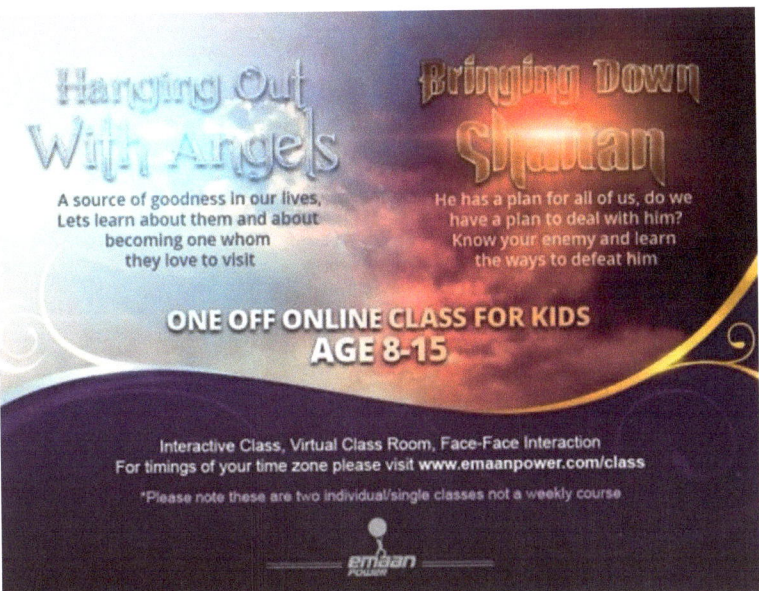
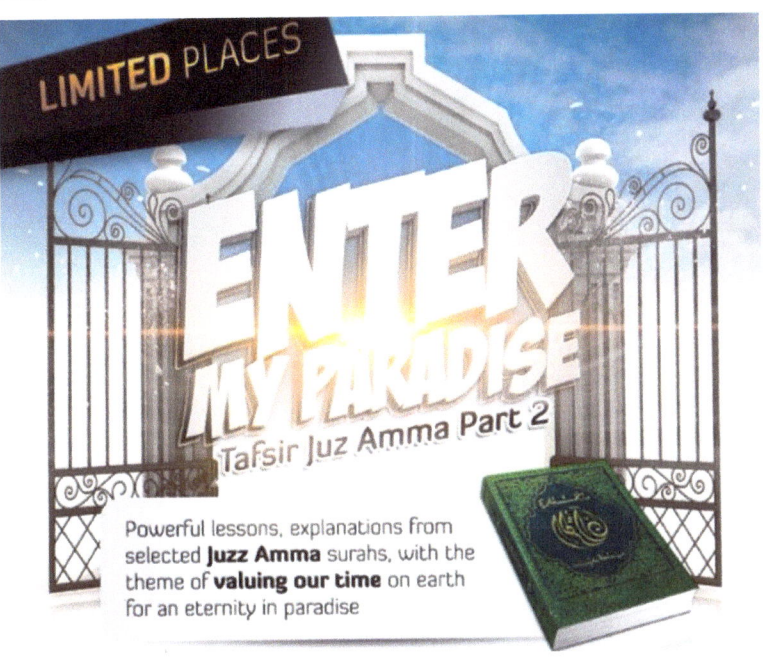

Emaan Power Video Packages, Books and CDs

You can reach us at

www.emaanpower.com

www.facebook.com/emaanpower

www.youtube/emaanpowerchannel

support@emaanpower.com

www.ingramcontent.com/pod-product-compliance
Lightning Source LLC
Chambersburg PA
CBHW042058290426
44113CB00001B/8